THE BIBLE OF

ALGORITHMS &
DATA STRUCTURES

A COMPLEX SUBJECT SIMPLY EXPLAINED

BY

FLORIAN DEDOV

Copyright © 2020

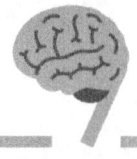

NeuralNine

Website: https://www.neuralnine.com/

Other Books: https://www.neuralnine.com/books

Instagram: https://www.instagram.com/NeuralNine

YouTube: https://www.youtube.com/c/NeuralNine

Github: https://github.com/NeuralNine

TABLE OF CONTENT

Introduction 6

    Why Learn All This? 7

    Structure of This Book 9

    Prerequisites 10

    YouTube Tutorials 11

1 – What Are Algorithms? 12

    Pseudocode 14

2 – What Are Data Structures? 17

    Interconnection 19

3 – Runtime Complexity 21

    What is Efficiency? 21

    What is Runtime? 22

    Runtime Complexity 24

    Asymptotic Growth 28

    Big-O Notation 31

        Omega Notation 36

        Theta Notation 37

    Important Runtimes 38

        Constant Time 38

        Logarithmic Time 40

        Linear Time 41

        Pseudo-Linear Time 42

        Quadratic Time 43

        Polynomial Time 45

        Exponential Time 46

Factorial Time 48
Analyzing Algorithms................................50
4 – Sorting Algorithms 57
Greedy Algorithms....................................57
Divide-And-Conquer Algorithms................58
Bubble Sort...59
Selection Sort 62
Insertion Sort 63
Merge Sort...66
Quick Sort...71
5 – Graph Theory & Algorithms 75
Graph Theory Basics................................75
Breadth First Search................................76
Depth First Search...................................79
Dijkstra Algorithm 81
Kruskal Algorithm 85
6 – Data Structures................................89
Linked List 89
Stack..92
Queue...94
Priority Queue...95
Heap...96
Binary Search Tree 101
7 – Self-Balancing Trees 105
AVL Tree 105
B-Tree..112
B*-Tree 120

8 – Hashing..122

   Hash Functions 124

      Division Method.....................................125

      Multiplication Method 126

   Collision Resolution...................................126

      Separate Chaining 127

      Open Addressing 128

      Linear Probing......................................129

      Quadratic Probing 131

      Double Hashing.....................................132

   What's Next? 134

INTRODUCTION

Algorithms and data structures are the nemesis of so many computer science students. It is a very abstract topic and it is oftentimes confusing for beginners. I personally think that one big reason for that is that it is oftentimes explained in a scientifically accurate but unnecessarily complex way. Most professors prefer textbook definitions rather than intuitive explanations. These are very important as well, because you need to be able to write down proofs and expressions in a scientifically accurate way. But especially at the beginning I think it is way better to focus on the intuition behind each concept first. Oftentimes it is easier to understand a complex concept using a metaphor, which is not 100% accurate but still good enough to give you the necessary understanding.

So that's what we are going to do in this book. Whenever we introduce a new concept, we will talk about it in a non-scientific way. We won't care about definitions that are mathematically correct 100%. The focus will be on getting an intuitive sense on what is happening. However, since scientifically valid definitions have their place, we will also work with those when they are beneficial and necessary. Sometimes we will use advanced mathematical notations and formal proofs. The main focus will nevertheless remain on the intuition of the concept.

Therefore this book cannot replace your university course or literature. It is more like a supplement for those who study computer science in college but also a great practical guide into algorithms and data structures for those who want to learn about this subject on their own. So if you just want to train your skills in this field on a practical level, without caring too much about all the formal details of mathematical notations, this book is a great choice for you.

WHY LEARN ALL THIS?

But before we get into it, let us answer a fundamental question here, that a lot of readers and students might be asking right now. Why should you learn all this? Why should anyone put effort into this subject, other than for passing the exam at college?

Let me give you a very practical reason first, before I get into the more technical stuff. Whenever you apply for a big software company as a programmer, database admin or networking expert, you will have a coding interview. And in most companies that you will probably want to work for (Apple, Google, Microsoft, Facebook...), you will most likely get a question based on algorithms and data structures. You will be presented an abstract problem that you need to solve efficiently. For this you will need to dissect the problem logically, use proper data structures and apply efficient algorithms. If you try to come up with an inefficient brute force solution, you will probably not get the job. Therefore, for this reason alone, it is reasonable to master the field of algorithms and data structures.

But some of you might not only be interested in a job or a degree. You might want to actually become a better programmer or a better computer scientist, just for the sake of it. And in this case, there is literally no way around algorithms and data structures. If you are a programmer, you need to solve problems in an efficient way. If you are an ethical hacker or a cyber security expert, you need to understand runtime complexity, hashing and cryptography. If you are into machine learning, you also need to be familiar with all these concepts. Generally speaking, programming is not about learning a language like Python, Java or C++. It is fundamentally about problem solving. When you are given a problem, most of the time there are numerous ways to solve it. If you have never heard about runtime complexity and algorithms, you will probably (if you are able to find any solution at all) come up with a very inefficient way of solving the problem. You can almost always brute force your way into a solution. The issue with that however is that for some (pretty medium-sized) problems, you will have to wait millions if not billions of years before they are solved. Learning about algorithms and data structures makes you a better problem solver and that is what a programmer or computer scientist fundamentally is. It is not someone who writes code into an editor. There are people on Fiverr and Wish who do that for 5$ an hour. If you don't want to be replaced by those guys, you better learn how to solve abstract problems efficiently.

STRUCTURE OF THIS BOOK

Now let us talk a little bit about how this book is structured and what you can expect. I already mentioned that our focus will be more on intuitive understanding, rather than on scientifically accurate definitions. For each concept we are going to start to learn about it by doing. We are going to use simple language and examples to understand what it is about. After that, if we decide it is useful, we might also cover the mathematically accurate formal definitions.

In the first few chapters, we will mainly talk about very fundamental and basic concepts. We will familiarize ourselves with the ideas of algorithms and data structures and we will look at how these two topics are interconnected. Also we will learn about runtime complexity, Big-O notation and analyzing algorithms. After that we will look at sorting algorithms and apply what we already know onto those. We will then get into the basics of graph theory, which is a fundamental mathematical subject of great importance in computer science. We will look at some interesting algorithms there. Later, we will mostly discuss the various different data structures there are and why you should or shouldn't use them in specific situations.

Generally speaking, we will work with a lot of examples and practical tasks. In my opinion that's the best way to learn about this subject. After reading this book, you should definitely be way more comfortable applying for a programming job or solving abstract and complex tasks in general.

PREREQUISITES

There are two basic prerequisites for this book. First of all, you should be familiar with basic coding principles. You should know your way around loops, if-statements, functions, variables, return values and you should have heard about recursion. These skills don't need to be in a particular language like Python or Java. A language is merely a tool. The concepts are what counts. This is important because we are going to work a lot with so-called *pseudocode*. This is code that is not limited to a particular syntax. It is easy to understand but only if you know these basic programming concepts. For the few practical coding examples in this book, we will be using Python, since it is the most similar to pseudocode.

If you want to brush up on your Python skills, you can also check out my book series called The Python Bible:
https://www.neuralnine.com/books

The second skill that you should have before reading this book is a high-school level understanding of math. I am not talking about partial differential equations here. I am talking about functions, logarithms, basic algebra, basic calculus etc. The only thing that you will maybe not have learned in high-school is the sigma sum notation. But we will briefly explain it in this book.

Other than that you are good to go. Of course this book will demand a lot of logical and abstract thinking from you. Sometimes it might take hours or days to wrap your mind around some of those ideas. But your success with this book is probably more dependent on your discipline and persistence that on your IQ level. So just don't get demotivated and keep pushing.

YOUTUBE TUTORIALS

Last but not least, you can also watch the YouTube videos on the NeuralNine YouTube channel, while reading this book. The videos are less structured and more free-flowing but the content is essentially the same. So if you are struggling with some of the content in written form, you might want to check out the respective free videos on YouTube.

Link: https://www.youtube.com/c/NeuralNine

I think you will get the best results if you combine the video content with the structured written content of this book. So let's get right into it and I wish you a lot of success and fun with this book.

1 – WHAT ARE ALGORITHMS?

The first question we need to ask is a very fundamental one: What are algorithms? If you want an exact textbook definition, check out the Wikipedia article on that. Here we are going to define them as *sets of instructions used to solve problems.* This is essentially what algorithms are. In this context a problem is basically just a synonym for task. A problem could be finding the shortest path from A to B, sorting a list or even more complex things like the knapsack problem or the traveling salesman problem. Also an algorithm doesn't have to be limited to a computer. It could also be executed by a human. Think about what you are doing when you are cooking a meal, you have never cooked before. You go online and download an algorithm (a set of instructions) called cooking recipe. Then you go through all the steps until the problem of cooking a meal is solved. However in the context of this book, we will obviously talk about computer algorithms most of the time. So let's look at a simple example. Imagine you have the following list of numbers:

8	5	7	2	1	9	4

The problem we have to solve here is sorting this list. As humans we can immediately see the right solution, because we recognize patterns, we have a big picture view and because the list is quite small. The correct solution is obviously the following:

1	2	4	5	7	8	9

But a computer cannot solve the problem just by looking at it and neither can we when the lists get larger. So we obviously need a specific set of instructions that solves this problem for us – an algorithm. Now there are multiple algorithms with different efficiencies and we are going to talk about those in depth in chapter four. But let's try to come up with one ourselves. What set of instructions could we give a computer in order to solve the problem of sorting a list?

One thing we could do is to just go through the whole list and find the smallest element. We can than swap this element with the element at the first position. In our case this would mean swapping 1 and 8.

1	5	7	2	8	9	4

We can then consider the first position to be correct, because it is definitely the smallest value. Since we can ignore the first position, we repeat the same process for the remaining six positions. The smallest element in there is the 2 and we swap it with the 5.

1	2	7	5	8	9	4

Now the first two positions are correct. We can continue this process until we end up with the sorted list. This way of sorting a list works on seven elements but it also works on a million elements. Is it efficient? Well, up until now we haven't really defined what efficient means so we cannot really answer that question. The set of instructions we just used is called *selection sort* and let's put it that way: it is not necessarily and algorithm that you would use very often for sorting a list. We will talk about efficiency in chapter three and we will cover this sorting algorithm in more detail during chapter four. For now I just wanted to show you an example of a basic algorithm that solves a basic problem.

PSEUDOCODE

The next step is to now put this algorithm into code. Up until now, we just described what we are doing with words, but we didn't write anything down as a set of instructions. Our goal is to put our procedure into code but at the same time this code shall be easy to understand and not limited to any language's syntax. For this we have pseudocode. Pseudocode doesn't have a particular fixed syntax. It is more like a code-like way of explaining what we do. The so-called *style* of your pseudocode can be C-like, Python-like or Pascal-like. It doesn't matter. However, we should still make sure we use certain keywords and we should definitely decide on a syntax for all the code in this book. Let's look at some variations of pseudocode before we do that.

```
a := 0
for x := 0 to 10:
    a = a + 1
    print(a)
```

```
a ← 0
  for x ← 0 until x ≥
10:
        a ← a + 1
        output(a)
```

```
a = 0
for(x = 0; x < 10; x++)
{
    a = a + 1;
    print(a);
}
```

```
a = 0
For x = 0 to 10 Do
    a = a + 1
    print(a)
End
```

As you can see, there are many different ways to write the same code. But now you might ask why we should even use pseudocode, when it is so similar to real code. The reason is that you are not limited to writing executable code. You can describe what you are doing with words and this allows you to focus on the logic of the algorithm. For this, let's look at the following example.

```
list := random list of numbers
even_counter := 0
five_counter := 0
for each number in list:
    if number is even:
        even_counter = evencounter + 1
    if number is divisible by five:
        five_counter = five_counter + 1
```

I hope you can see what I mean. Even though we are still looking at actual code, we can oftentimes describe what we are doing in words. Instead of initializing a randomizer and creating random values, I can just say that I am creating a list of random numbers, since the focus of this algorithm is not on randomizing values. Also instead of using the modulus operator I can just check for *even* or *divisible by five*. Throughout this book I am going to use this Python-like pseudocode style. Feel free to choose any other style if you don't like this one though.

Pseudocode will not only be important so that we can write down algorithms. We will also look at pseudocode to analyze the runtime complexity of an algorithm, which is the topic of chapter three. But before we get into that, we need to talk about data structures as well.

2 – WHAT ARE DATA STRUCTURES?

Algorithms and data structures are two topics that are almost always taught together. You will rarely find two separate courses on these two subjects because they are deeply interconnected. Algorithms make use of data structures and data structures need algorithms to function. But before we talk about this in more detail, let us answer the question of what a data structure actually is.

Essentially it is just a format for storing, managing, working with or (as the name already suggests) structuring data or information. Every data structure comes with its own set of advantages and disadvantages. Even though we are not going to talk about the individual data structures in detail yet (this is the topic of chapter six), we will briefly look at an example. For this we will compare an ordinary array with a so-called linked list.

Let's say we have an array of size six that looks like this:

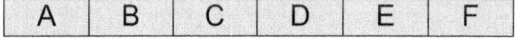

| A | B | C | D | E | F |

If we are now interested in knowing the value at position number four (index three), we can access this position in so-called *constant time* (more about this in the next chapter). We just have to calculate the memory address and access it. This is one of the advantages that an array has. Accessing elements is very efficient. On the other hand however, we have the disadvantage that an array has a fixed size. Of course during the initialization we can choose an arbitrarily high size but this size remains fixed and static after that. We cannot just make an array smaller or larger in terms of memory size.

This works differently with linked lists. Without going too much into details here, linked lists are basically structured in the following way: We have multiple nodes, each consisting of a value and a pointer. The pointer of one node always points to a next node. Only the pointer of the last node is pointing to null.

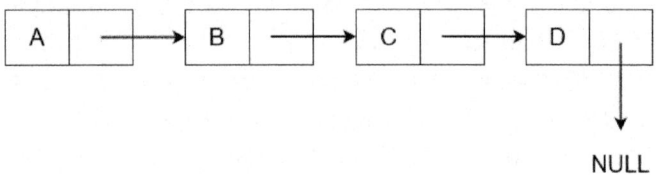

Fig. 2.1: Structure of a linked list

This structure allows for a dynamic sizing. In order to increase the size, all we need to do is create a new node and squish it into the list by adjusting the pointers. Decreasing the size is done by simply removing a node and closing the gaps with the pointers.

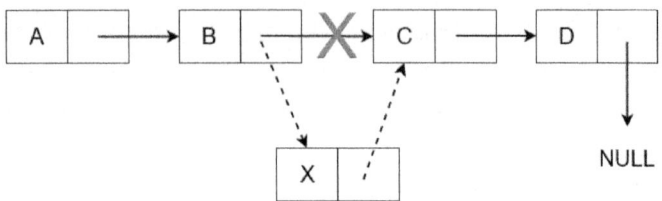

Fig. 2.2: Adding a new node to a linked list

But there is another problem with linked lists. Since you can add and remove nodes at any point in time, the memory address structure is not static. In order to access an element, we need to access the pointer of the previous element (unless it is the first one). But to access this previous element, you need to use the pointer of the element before that and so on. This essentially means that you need to iterate through each node that comes before your "goal node" in order to access it. Accessing an element is no longer possible in constant time. It is less efficient in linked lists than in arrays.

As you can see, for different problems we will use different data structures. Sometimes we won't care about dynamic sizing because we exactly know how many slots we will need and that this number will not change. Sometimes we can't accept a static size and thus we won't be able to use ordinary arrays. Also, there are numerous other data structures like binary search trees, stacks and heaps, which all have their use-cases.

INTERCONNECTION

And this brings us to the interconnection between algorithms and data structures. Algorithms are used to solve problems and for some problems we need to structure the given data efficiently. Sometimes we might be given a set of numbers, which has to be processed in a queue-like manner. For this we can use the priority queue data structure or a stack. Sometimes we will want to search for values efficiently, so we will structure the data in a binary search tree. The point is the following: Algorithms make use of data structures in order to solve problems more efficiently. Of course we could always just use arrays for each problem, but we would sacrifice a lot of speed then.

But the interconnection is not a one-way street. Data structures work with algorithms all the time. Remember that we defined algorithms as sets of instructions used to solve problems. Data structures are full of problems. Problems like accessing, deleting, finding, inserting etc. Inserting an element into a linked list demands a different set of instructions than inserting it into an ordinary array. For some data structures these fundamental operations are quite complex, since a certain format needs to be maintained.

Now you should have a basic understanding of what we are studying here and why it is important. In the next chapter we will talk about some real analysis of algorithms.

3 – RUNTIME COMPLEXITY

One of the most important topics when it comes to algorithms is *runtime complexity*. Maybe you have heard some statements like "This problem can be solved in linear time" or "This algorithm has a quadratic runtime complexity". In this chapter we are going to demystify these statements and learn how to determine the runtime complexity of algorithms.

WHAT IS EFFICIENCY?

The first question we need to answer here is: What is efficiency? When we say that an algorithm is more efficient than another one, what does that mean? Does it mean that it is faster? Yes, kind of but what does that mean? To answer that question, let's look at some possible metrics for efficiency:

- Memory space needed
- Runtime of the algorithm
- Problem-specific metrics (i.e.: amount of comparisons made by sorting algorithms)

Think about it: If an algorithm A solves a problem in 20 minutes but needs 2 TB of memory to do so, is it more efficient than an algorithm B that solves the problem in 4 hours while using 20 GB? Well it depends on what you care more about. Although we could also analyze algorithms in terms of memory space allocated, in this book our focus will mostly be on the runtime of algorithms.

WHAT IS RUNTIME?

But this brings us to the next question: What is runtime? Let's start by working with a naïve definition and see what kinds of problems we run into. We could say that runtime is just the amount of seconds, minutes or time units in general that an algorithm needs to solve a problem. And actually that is a correct definition but it won't help us to determine the efficiency of an algorithm.

For this let's look at an imaginary example. Let's say we have two computers A and B, which both solve the same problem with two different algorithms X and Y.

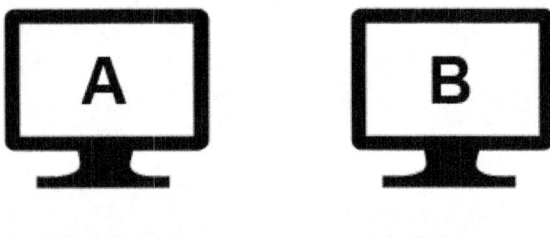

X: 10 Minutes   Y: 5 Hours

Fig 3.1: Thought experiment

Now if computer A solves the problem, using algorithm X, in ten minutes and computer B solves it, using algorithm Y, in five hours, what does this tell us about the efficiency of the individual algorithms? The answer is: not much, if anything at all. Computer A could be a high end computer, computer B could be a computer from the year 1990 and the problem size could be too small to matter.

So why not try both algorithms on the same machine? There are still multiple problems with this idea. First of all, we will not always have the same runtime, even if we use the same algorithm and the same problem instance. There are many (almost) random factors outside of our control that influence the performance of the machine. Also, sometimes one algorithm solves a problem faster than another one, but only as long as the problem size doesn't get too big. After a certain size the other algorithm may be more efficient. But there is another problem as well. Even if all these things wouldn't matter, it would be virtually impossible to have one central machine, where everyone can run their algorithms to determine the "objective" runtime, in order to compare it to others.

Because of this, we analyze algorithms on paper and assume a simplified model for our computer. The constraints are the following:

- Our computer has only a single CPU
- All the data is stored in the RAM
- Every memory access requires the exact same amount of time

The first point is important because we don't want to take concurrency and multi-processing into account. The second and third point are important because we don't want to deal with the hardware differences of how long it takes to access data in the RAM and on the hard drive.

RUNTIME COMPLEXITY

Now we can use this simplified model and analyze the efficiency of algorithms by looking at their runtime complexity. The difference between runtime and runtime complexity is that we are not looking at time units but at the amount of so-called *primitive operations.* We define those in a simplified way to make the analysis of algorithms easier. It is very hard to examine the exact runtime complexity of a set of instructions. There are just too many hardware and environmental factors involved. However we don't need to do it. All we care about is how efficient the logic of the algorithm is. So what we do is we call most basic instructions primitive and say that they all require the same amount of time (even though they actually don't exactly). Examples for primitive operations are the following:

- Assigning a value to a variable
- Arithmetic operations
- Logical operations
- If-statements and comparisons
- Some more…

Basically everything that doesn't have a complex algorithm behind it can be considered primitive. This works for us since we are not interested in small differences. We don't care if a multiplication takes a little bit longer than an addition or an assignment. Those differences don't influence the efficiency of the logic too much. So we neglect them.

However, since we are working with pseudocode, we may encounter some instructions that are not primitive but quite complex. Let's look at an example.

```
list := [list of random numbers]
sort list using merge sort
for each element in list:
    print(element)
```

We can consider printing an element a primitive operation, if we want to. However initializing a list of random numbers and sorting it is definitely not primitive. Merge sort has a runtime complexity of **n $log(n)$**. We are going to talk about what that means in a second. What you need to understand for now is that we need to read through every line of pseudocode carefully when we analyze an algorithm, because one line doesn't necessarily equal one primitive instruction. But let's actually go ahead and try to determine the runtime complexity of a simple algorithm.

```
list = [list of n numbers]
a := 0
for each element in list:
    a = a + 1
    print(a)
```

Essentially what this algorithm does is iterating over a list of numbers, increasing a counter and printing all the values. Let's interpret the first line as just assigning a list to a variable instead of generating a new one. In this case it can be seen as a primitive operation. The second line is also a primitive operation, since we just assign a value to a variable. Then we get into a for loop. The code of the for loop is executed once for each element in the list. Since the list has n elements, the code runs n times. Inside the loop we just have two more primitive operations.

```
list = [list of n numbers] (1 PO)
a := 0 (1 PO)
for each element in list: (n times)
    a = a + 1 (1 PO)
    print(a) (1 PO)
```

So if we want to calculate the runtime complexity of the script we just need to add the first two operations to n times the second two operations. The result would then be:

$$2 + 2n$$

As you can see, the runtime complexity is not just a number but a function. It depends on the input size n. If we have 20 elements, we will have 42 primitive operations. If we have 100 elements, we will execute 202 primitive operations.

But even that is not always the case. Let's add an additional line to our pseudocode to make things a bit more complicated.

```
list = [list of n numbers] (1 PO)
a := 0 (1 PO)
for each element in list: (n times)
    if element is even: (1 PO)
        a = a + 1 (1 PO)
        print(a) (1 PO)
```

The additional line we added is just an if-statement that checks if the current element is even. It only executes the last two instructions, when this is the case. But what is the runtime complexity of this algorithm now? When all values are even, we have way more operations than when all values are odd. And most likely we will have a mix of both, so how can we calculate the amount of primitive operations here?

For this we can look at three different runtime complexities: The best-case, the average-case and the worst-case complexity. The best case is the scenario, in which we have a list that produces the least amount of operations. In this example, this would be a list full of odd numbers. We would then execute the first two instructions and the loop would still run n times. However, we would only execute one instruction inside of the loop, namely the if-statement. So the best-case runtime complexity of this algorithm would be:

$$2 + n$$

The worst case on the other hand is when all numbers are even and we enter the if-block every single time. In this scenario the runtime complexity would be:

$$2 + 3n$$

But what about the average-case complexity? Isn't it the most relevant? In a sense it is but it is also very hard to calculate. Of course if you know that the numbers are totally random, you can assume a 50/50 split and the complexity would be:

$$2 + 3\frac{n}{2} + \frac{n}{2} = 2 + \frac{4n}{2} = 2 + 2n$$

But in reality you will rarely be able to calculate a solid average-case runtime complexity. Most of the time, you will focus on the worst-case complexity. As computer scientists we are not really interested too much in what can go right in special cases. We want to know how bad things can get in the worst case. So when you hear that an algorithm solves a problem in linear, quadratic or whatever time, this most-likely refers to the worst-case scenario.

ASYMPTOTIC GROWTH

Most of the time, it will be very hard to calculate the exact amount of primitive operations needed to solve a problem. Oftentimes it is virtually impossible. So what we are actually interested in is the *asymptotic growth* of the function. For this, we will use the following principles:

- We don't care about small instances of problems
- We don't care about constant summands
- We don't care about constant factors

In a nutshell: Our focus is solely on how strong the runtime is growing, when we add new elements to the problem. We are not interested in exact values. We are interested the type of growth.

Let's look at a simple example. If we have a linear function with a constant factor of 3000, the slope of the function would be pretty high but the type of growth would still be linear. For every additional element we add to the problem, we need to perform 3000 additional steps. On the other hand, having a quadratic function with a constant factor of 0.1 might be growing very slowly in the beginning but over time it will outgrow the linear function, because the growth is quadratic. The same is true for constant values that we add to the function. If a linear or even constant function starts at one million, it will still be outgrown sooner or later by a quadratic function that starts at zero. The following graph should illustrate this concept pretty well.

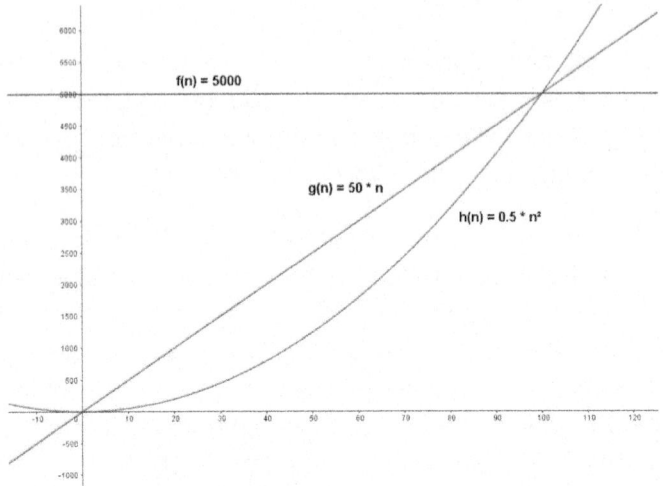

Fig 3.2: Runtime complexities visualized

As you can see, in the graph above we have three different functions that represent runtime complexities. The first one is a constant function, which means that it doesn't grow. It constantly stays at 5000 primitive operations, no matter how big the problem instance gets. Because of that, you can see that it is the worst choice in the beginning. If we are dealing with a small size, this runtime complexity is the most inefficient. Then we also have a linear function with a constant factor of 50. Notice that the coordinate system has a different scale on the x-axis than on the y-axis. You can see that this function is growing quite fast in the beginning. It needs more operations than the quadratic runtime complexity. So for the first hundred elements, the quadratic runtime is the most "efficient". However this changes when we get to higher numbers. The constant function will remain at 5000 operations, no matter how large problem size gets. Because of that it will always be the most efficient runtime complexity from a certain point onwards. The linear function might be growing fast in the beginning, but n^2 is quadratic and essentially means $n * n$. This means that at some point n will get larger than every constant factor you can come up with. No matter which constants you choose, at some point the quadratic function will be less efficient than the constant and linear functions. And it will never be outgrown by these again. The key point here is that all these constants do not matter, because we only care about the general type of growth. We don't care about small problem instances, since these are manageable most of the time. We want to know which algorithm is the best, when we scale the problem size up. Constant time will never be beaten by linear time in the long run. And linear time will never be outperformed by quadratic time no matter how large the constants get. We will take a look at the different types of growth later in this chapter.

BIG-O NOTATION

Now things will get a little bit more mathematical. When we talk about the runtime complexity of algorithms in a mathematical context, we will almost always use the so-called *Big-O notation*. This notation essentially gives us information about how some functions limit other functions. Let's look at a simple example.

If we have a function n^2 and a function *100n*, at some point the function n^2 is going to serve as an upper boundary for the *100n* function. The linear function will always stay below n^2, once a certain value for n is passed. Put into more mathematical words:

$$\exists\, N > 0: \quad \forall n > N: \quad n^2 > 100n$$

This essentially means that there is a starting index N, after which for each n that is larger than N the n^2 function dominates the *100n* function. In this case this N is obviously 100. However, when we use the Big-O notation, we can take things even further. We can multiply the function we want to try to use as an upper boundary by any constant we want. If the inequality is then true for infinitely many values, we can use the following notation:

$$100n = O(n^2)$$

The full mathematical definition is the following:

$$\exists N > 0 \wedge \exists C > 0: \quad \forall n > N: \quad f(n) < g(n) * C$$
$$\rightarrow f(n) = O\big(g(n)\big)$$

Don't give up yet. It is not as difficult as it looks. Let me put it into English words for you: If there is a starting index N and an arbitrary constant C (both larger than zero) so that for all n that are larger than this starting index, the function f is always smaller than the function g multiplied by this constant, we can say that f is in Big-O of g.

Let me try to explain this even simpler: If a function g, multiplied by an arbitrarily chosen constant, outgrows a function f at any point in the coordinate system (forever), we can say that f is in Big-O of g.

Let's look at a practical example:

$$f(n) = 20n^2 + 5n + 10 \qquad g(n) = n^2$$

Obviously, as long as n stays positive, f is always going to return a larger value than g. But this doesn't matter. We want to analyze the asymptotic relationship. So if we can find a constant and a starting index, so that the mathematical condition above is met, we can still say that f is bounded above by g.

Let's think about it. No matter how large the constant we choose is, when n equals zero, f will always be larger than g, since it has the constant summand ten. So let's choose one as our starting index N. Now which factor, would we need to choose for C, in order to always have a larger value on the right?

$$20n^2 + 5n + 10 < n^2 * C \qquad (n \geq 1)$$

Let's just divide both sides by n^2. Then we can try to figure out the minimum value for C.

$$20 + \frac{5}{n} + \frac{10}{n} < C \qquad (n \geq 1)$$

Now we can see that the C has to be larger than the expression on the left side. But there is the variable n, so what can we do about it? Since our starting value for n is one and it is only going to increase, we can see that the value of the fractions is going to decrease, since n is in the denominator. This means that the highest value on the left side is the one that we get when n equals one. After that it will only get smaller.

$$20 + \frac{5}{1} + \frac{10}{1} = 35 < C$$

So as you can see, C has to be larger than 35. Let us just choose 36 as our constant. We can now check visually if this solution is right.

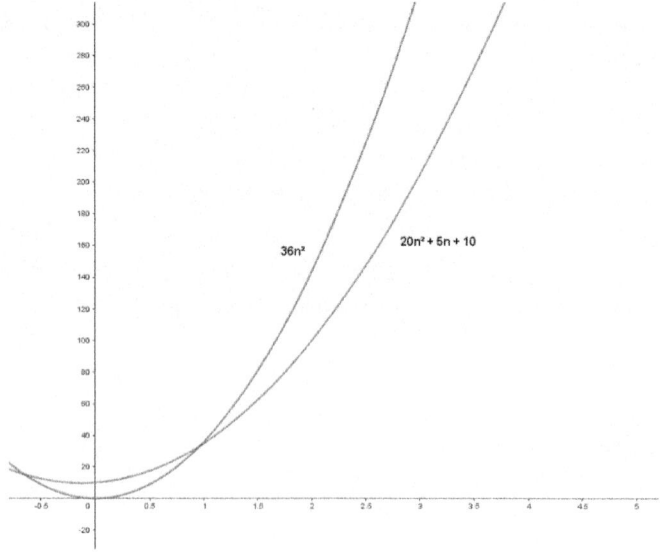

Fig 3.3: Visualization of the result

In the figure above you can see that at around n = 1, our newly constructed function outgrows the given function. It is bounding it above. Therefore *f* is in Big-O of *g*.

$$20n^2 + 5n + 10 = O(n^2)$$

But now you might ask: Doesn't this always work? Can't we always find a constant and a starting point and isn't therefore every function in $O(n^2)$? The answer is no and we will look at one more example to see why that is the case.

$$f(n) = n^3 + 2n \qquad g(n) = n^2$$

Here the function *f* is a polynomial of third three and *g* is a polynomial of degree two. Let's just try to pick a high starting index like 100. Now we would have to find a constant C by solving the following inequality.

$$n^3 + 2n < n^2 * C \qquad (n \geq 100)$$

So let's again try to divide both sides by n² in order to isolate our constant.

$$n + \frac{2}{n} < C \qquad (n \geq 100)$$

Since, our starting index is 100, the fraction is negligible. It won't make much of a difference. So even though it is not 100% mathematically correct, let's just ignore it. We will still run into problems, don't worry.

$$n < C \qquad (n \geq 100)$$

You might start to see the problem here. In order to show that *f* is in Big-O of *g*, we need to find a constant that is larger than n. But n starts at 100 and goes off into infinity. This means that we need to find a constant that is larger than any other natural number. This is not possible. Because of that, we can say that *f* is definitely not in Big-O of *g*.

If you want to look at it in a simpler way, you could say that it is obvious that n³ can never be bounded above by n² no matter which constants you choose, since n³ is growing faster than n² and the additional factor n, will always exceed any given constant.

Omega Notation

The whole magic works for lower boundaries as well. If we want to say that a function is bounded below by another function, we use the *omega notation* instead of the Big-O notation.

$$f(n) = \ \Omega(g(n))$$

To define when a function is in omega of another function, we use the same inequality, we used for Big-O but this time we change the "smaller" sign to a "larger" sign.

$$\exists N > 0 \ \wedge \ \exists C > 0: \quad \forall n > N: \ f(n) > g(n) * C$$
$$\rightarrow f(n) = \Omega\big(g(n)\big)$$

Again this notation just means that, if we can find a small enough constant and a starting index for which this inequality is true, we can use the omega notation.

Let's look at an example again:

$$f(n) = n^2 \qquad g(n) = 200 * n^2$$

Here we want to show that *200 * n²* serves as a lower boundary of *n²*. In order to do that, we need to find a small enough constant and a starting point, for which this is the case. Let's just pick zero as a starting point and find a constant, which satisfies the inequality.

$$n^2 > 200 * n^2 * C \qquad (n \geq 0)$$

$$1 > 200 * C \qquad (n \geq 0)$$

$$\frac{1}{200} > C \qquad (n \geq 0)$$

Applying the same steps as always, we can see that if we choose a constant, which is smaller than one over 200, the function *g* is a lower boundary of the function *f*. This is obviously the case, since the fraction cancels out the factor of 200. If the denominator increases, the function on the right will get even smaller.

THETA NOTATION

With the knowledge you now have you might have noticed than some functions serve as an upper and as a lower boundary for the same function. When this is the case both functions are asymptotically equivalent and we have a special notation for this – the *theta notation*.

$$f(n) = O\big(g(n)\big) \land f(n) = \Omega(g(n))$$

$$\rightarrow f(n) = \theta(n)$$

Roughly speaking, for polynomials, you can say that two functions are asymptotically equal, when their degree is the same.

IMPORTANT RUNTIMES

Now you should have a pretty decent understanding of what runtime is and how to use the individual notations. So next we are going to take a look at the most common and most important runtime complexities you might encounter and how they come into existence. We will start with the most efficient and work our way up to the most inefficient algorithmic complexities.

CONSTANT TIME

We already talked about constant time in this chapter. Constant runtime complexity doesn't grow. The same amount of steps is needed no matter how large the input size gets. Here it doesn't matter if the constant amount is one or five thousand. Remember: Constants are irrelevant! When we want to say that an algorithm solves a problem in constant time, we can do this by using the Big-O or the theta notation.

$O(1)$ $\theta(1)$

Fig. 3.4: Constant time

Since constants do not matter, we can use the number one to represent all constant runtime complexities. But how could constant time come into existence? Let's look at a very simple example. You have a linked list and you want to print the value of the element at index six. For this you need to iterate over the first six elements and then print the value of the next element. This is a procedure that takes the same amount of steps, no matter how large the list actually is. It won't get more complicated just because the list has a trillion elements. You still need to do the same steps. So the runtime complexity of this is constant.

Logarithmic Time

You probably remember the logarithmic function from high school. In a nutshell it tells you how many times you have to multiply the base by itself to get the given number as a result. So the logarithm base two of 32 is five because two to the power of five is 32.

Usually we encounter logarithmic time whenever the problem size is halved with each iteration. A binary search in a sorted list is a perfect example for this. Don't worry if you don't know what this is. We will talk about it in another chapter.

$$O(\log n) \qquad \theta(\log n)$$

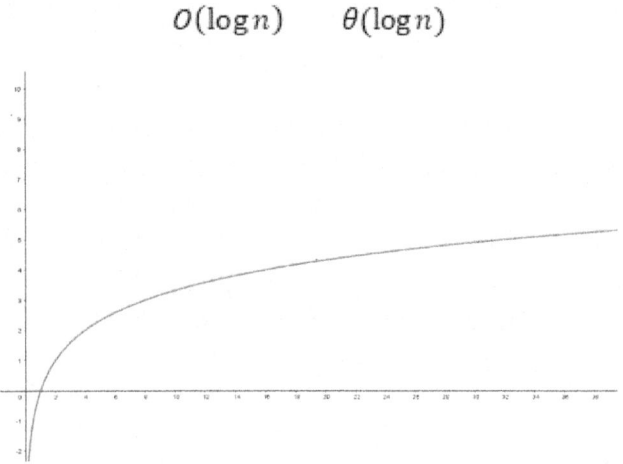

Fig. 3.5: Logarithmic time

The good thing about logarithmic time is that its growth is slowing down over time. So the curve gets flatter and flatter as we go on. When you get to really high numbers the graph looks almost like a constant runtime complexity. If a problem can be solved in logarithmic time, you cannot really consider it a problem. It is extremely efficient.

LINEAR TIME

Less efficient but still nothing you would ever complain about is linear time complexity. This essentially means that the growth is constant. For each additional unit in the problem size, we need the same amount of extra steps. The growth doesn't depend on the problem size.

An example for linear time would be finding the maximum value of an unsorted list. You need to go through each element in order to get your result. More elements in the list means more iterations and comparisons.

$$O(n) \qquad \theta(n)$$

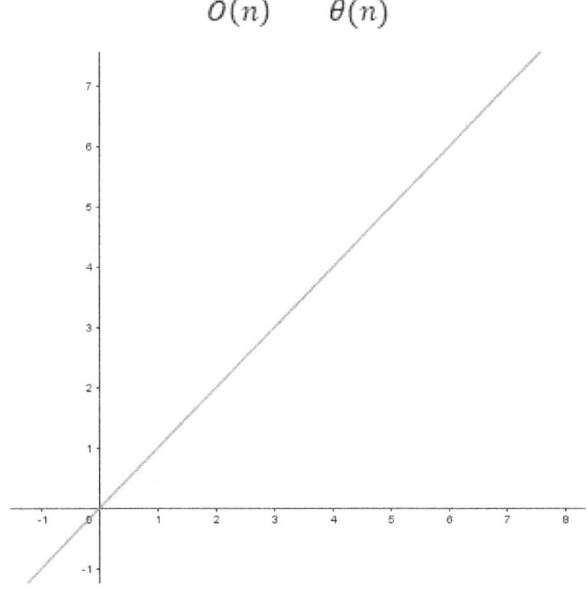

Fig. 3.6: Linear time

If a problem is solvable in linear time it is also not really a challenge. It is very easy to solve and the runtime complexity is extremely desirable. However, most problems cannot be solved in linear time (at least we haven't found any ways to do it yet).

PSEUDO-LINEAR TIME

Now if we combine the last two runtime complexities (logarithmic and linear), we get the *pseudo-linear* time. It is sometimes also called *linearithmic.*

This time complexity is oftentimes found in *divide-and-conquer* algorithms. We will encounter this runtime when we get to more advanced sorting algorithms like merge sort, quick sort and heap sort.

$$O(n \log n) \qquad \theta(n \log n)$$

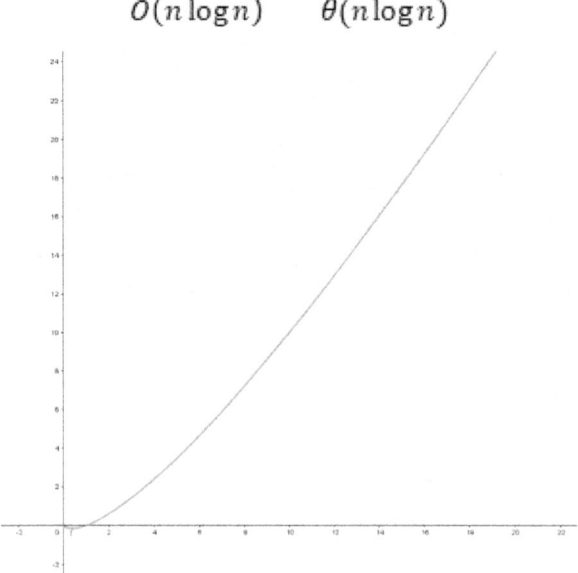

Fig. 3.7: Pseudo-linear time

As you can see, the function is not quite linear but since the logarithmic part grows slower and slower over time, it looks like one when we get to larger numbers. This is the last runtime complexity that we will consider very efficient. If a problem is solvable in *n log n* time, it is not really a challenge.

QUADRATIC TIME

Now we get to runtime complexities that are still considered efficient and manageable but only when compared to exponential and factorial time.

Quadratic time means that the amount of steps is not only increasing when we add new elements to the problem instance but it is also increasing faster the more elements we already have. This was also true for pseudo-linear time, but now we can actually notice it.

Examples for quadratic runtime are inefficient sorting algorithms like bubble sort, insertion sort or selection sort but also traversing a simple 2D array.

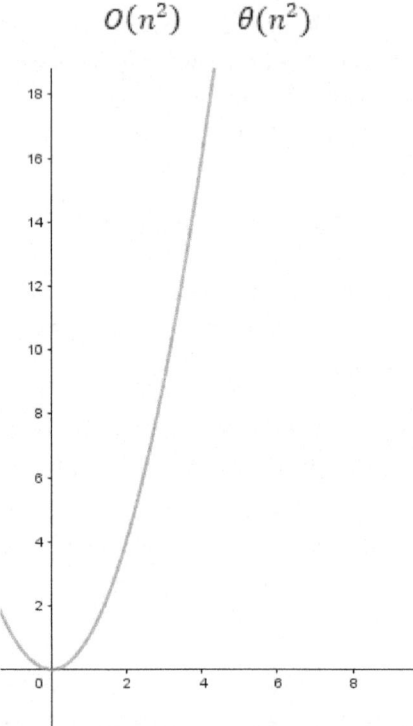

Fig. 3.8: Quadratic time

You can see that the growth is happening a lot faster here. It is still manageable, but quadratic runtime can be a challenge sometimes.

POLYNOMIAL TIME

Generally-speaking polynomial time is the last thing that we can consider manageable. Of course if the exponent gets too high, it is also a problem, but still nothing compared to exponential growth.

$$O(n^k) \qquad \theta(n^k)$$

So whenever we have a runtime complexity of n to the power of k (k is a constant), we are dealing with polynomial runtime complexity.

EXPONENTIAL TIME

What you definitely want to avoid is exponential runtime complexity. Even if you are not a math genius, you probably know that exponential growth is happening extremely fast.

Examples for problems that can (at least for now) only be solved in exponential time are brute forcing passwords and finding subset sums in a set of numbers.

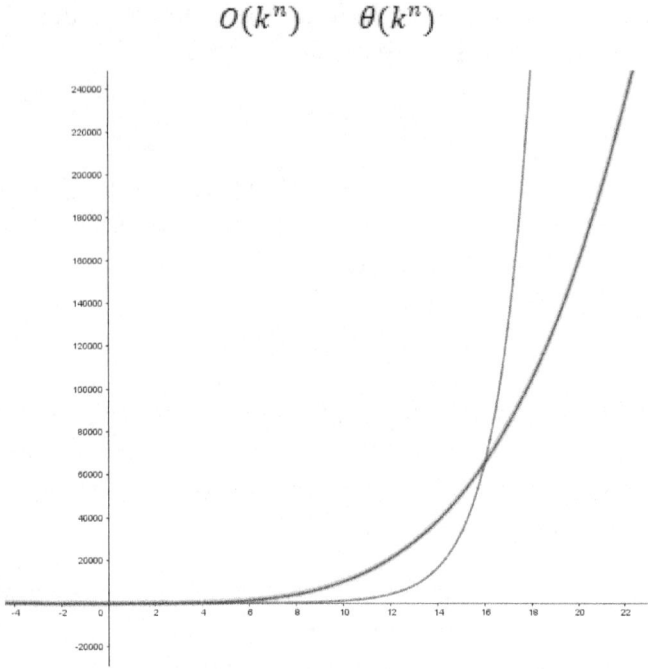

Fig. 3.9: Exponential time compared to polynomial time

Notice that the Big-O and theta notation of exponential time is the same as the one for polynomial time, except for the fact that the base and the exponent are swapped. Now the base is constant and the exponent is depending on the input size.

In the graph above you can see how the exponential function with base two outgrows the polynomial function n to the power of four rapidly. Notice the scale of both axes here. The input sizes are pretty small, but the operations needed grow extremely fast. Whenever it is possible, you want to avoid exponential runtime complexity.

FACTORIAL TIME

Last but not least we also have factorial time. This time complexity is even less desirable than exponential time. Let me refresh your knowledge about the factorial function real quick. The definition is the following:

$$n! = n * (n - 1) * (n - 2) * ... * 3 * 2 * 1$$

We basically multiply n by all natural numbers that are smaller than n except for zero. One runtime complexity that is worse than that is of the form n to the power of n, but it almost never occurs.

However factorial time does occur. For example, when you try to find all possible permutations of a given set of elements. But there is also a very practical and important problem that is solved in factorial time – the *travelling salesman* problem. Although there is a dynamic programming solution (advanced topic not covered in this book) to this problem, which is more efficient, the naïve approach solves the problem in factorial time.

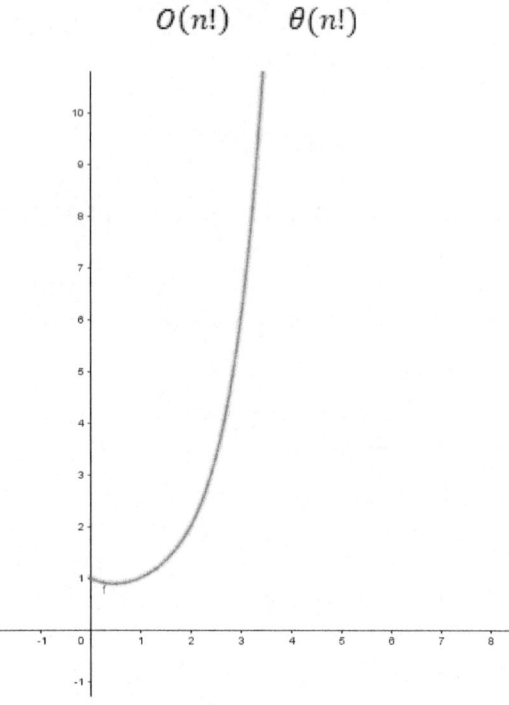

Fig. 3.10: Factorial time

I think it goes without saying that you want to avoid factorial time whenever it is possible. We don't consider this time complexity manageable.

Now you should have a decent overview over the most important runtime complexities and how they come into existence. You should also have a little bit of an intuition about which complexities are manageable and desirable and which are not.

ANALYZING ALGORITHMS

For the last part of this chapter, we are going to analyze some actual algorithms. We will apply the knowledge that we now have and determine their runtime complexity. Understanding these concepts is one thing. Being able to apply them is another. So let us get into the examples:

Algorithm A

```
k := 0
for i = 1 to n:
    for j = (i + 1) to n:
        k = k + j + i
return k
```

Yes this example is way harder than the ones we already did. But that's good, since we want to improve our abstract thinking abilities. Now here there are two things that we will want to look at. The first one is the runtime complexity of the algorithm and the second one is a formula for the return value k. Let's try to analyze this line-by-line.

```
k := 0 (1 PO)
for i = 1 to n: (n times)
    for j = (i + 1) to n: (???)
        k = k + j + i (1 PO)
return k (1 PO)
```

The first and the last line can be ignored, since they just add a constant (two steps) to the result. Inside of the second loop, we have only one operation, so nothing too complex. The tricky question however is: How many times do we run through the second loop? It constantly changes. Let's try to find a pattern.

The variable i starts at one. So the first time it runs from two to n. Since i is constantly increasing, it runs from three to n, then from four to n and so on.

```
(n-1) times, (n-2) times, (n-3) times...
```

So we could say that the total amount of iterations is just the sum of the pattern above. It would look like this:

$$(n - 1) + (n - 2) + (n - 3) + \cdots + 3 + 2 + 1 + 0$$

We can now use the sigma sum notation to write this in a more mathematical way.

$$\sum_{i=1}^{n} (n - i) = (n - 1) + (n - 2) + \cdots + (n - n)$$

This notation works a little bit like a for loop. We just specify a control variable and a starting index. Then we iterate over all values between this starting index and n and sum up all the results. The expression on the left can then be re-written into a formula. If you don't know how to do this, don't worry. This is not the subject of this book. You can either use online tools like Wolfram Alpha to find solutions or just memorize them. Alternatively of course, you can learn how to find these formulas yourself.

$$\sum_{i=1}^{n} (n - i) = \frac{n * (n - 1)}{2}$$

Whatever method you use, this is the result that you should get. And using this, we can now determine the runtime complexity of the algorithm. This is the amount of primitive operations executed by both loops. It tells us how many times we enter the second loop in total and execute the primitive operation inside. So let's multiply out the brackets.

$$\frac{n * (n - 1)}{2} = \frac{1}{2} * (n^2 - n)$$

As we already know, constant factors are irrelevant. Therefore we can ignore the fraction. After that, it is obvious that our runtime complexity is quadratic.

$$n^2 - n = \theta(n^2)$$

But what about the return value? Can we come up with a formula for it as well? Of course we can and we will. But since the main focus on this book is on algorithmic complexity, we will go through this a bit faster and consider it an "extra task" for those who are more interested. So feel free to skip to the second algorithm, if you are not interested in this.

We can see that the values we add change every time. So let's look at the i and the j values separately.

The *i* value is quite simple. We know that we add it (n − i) times.

$$1 * (n - 1) + 2 * (n - 2) + 3 * (n - 3) \ldots$$

Now we can just rewrite this, using the sigma notation again:

$$\sum_{i=1}^{n} i * (n - i) = \frac{(n+1) * n * (n - 1)}{6}$$

When we multiply this out, we get a third degree polynomial.

$$\frac{(n+1) * n * (n - 1)}{6} = \frac{1}{6} * (n^3 - n)$$

Next we will look at the *j* variable. This one is a little bit more complicated. It is constantly changing. But when we think about it, we see that we are adding the values from 2 to n a different amount of times. The number 2 is only added once, the number 3 twice, the number 4 three times and so on. So *j* is always added *j* − *1* times. This pattern can again be written as a sigma sum.

$$\sum_{j=2}^{n} j * (j - 1) = \frac{(n+1) * n * (n - 1)}{3}$$

Now we just need to add these two results together and we have a formula for our return value *k*.

$$\frac{(n+1)*n*(n-1)}{6} + \frac{(n+1)*n*(n-1)}{3} =$$

$$\frac{(n+1)*n*(n-1)}{6} + \frac{2*(n+1)*n*(n-1)}{6} =$$

$$\frac{3*(n+1)*n*(n-1)}{6} = \frac{(n+1)*n*(n-1)}{2} =$$

$$\frac{n^3 - n}{2} = \theta(n^3)$$

As I already said, don't worry if you don't get this part. It is not fundamental for the rest of the book. I picked more difficult examples so that you get used to more complex stuff.

Algorithm B

```
k := 0
i := 2ⁿ
while i > 0:
    k = k + i²
    i = ⌊i/2⌋
return k
```

Now let's look at this second algorithm. As you can see it has a very different structure. Instead of two for loops, we have one while loop and instead of starting with zero and increasing up to a max value, we start with an exponential expression and halve its size in each iteration. Let's start again by analyzing it line-by-line.

```
k := 0 (1 PO)
i := 2^n (1 PO)
while i > 0: (???)
    k = k + i² (1 PO)
    i = ⌊i/2⌋ (1 PO)
```

So the only mystery here is, how many times the loop gets executed. The loop gets executed over and over again until the variable *i* hits zero or a smaller value. Now if we look at the initialization of this variable, we can see that it is two to the power of n. This means two multiplied by itself n times. Inside the loop, we divide this value by two in each iteration. Because of that we obviously need to divide this value n times to get to one and then one more time to get to a value, which we can floor to zero. So the loop runs n + 1 times.

```
k := 0 (1 PO)
i := 2^n (1 PO)
while i > 0: (n + 1 times)
    k = k + i² (1 PO)
    i = ⌊i/2⌋ (1 PO)
```

We can therefore say that this algorithm has linear runtime complexity and is in theta of n – *θ(n)*. Now let us again (for those readers who are interested) take a look at the return value *k*. We are essentially just adding *i²* every time. But the value of *i* is halved with each iteration. So we could write down the following sum.

$$k = (2^n)^2 + (2^{n-1})^2 + (2^{n-2})^2 + \cdots$$

Using the sigma sum notation this can be written as:

$$\sum_{i=0}^{n} \left(2^{n-i}\right)^2 = \frac{4^{n+1} - 1}{3}$$

We can now extract a four out of the numerator and then ignore it, since it is a constant factor. We can also ignore the denominator and the negative one. What we end up with is the following:

$$4 * \frac{4^n - 1}{3} \quad \rightarrow \quad \theta(4^n)$$

So the formula for our return value is an exponential function.

This chapter was quite mathematical and demanding. Don't give up if you didn't understand everything 100%. Some things are just good to know and not needed for the rest of the book. The goal of this chapter was only to give you an understanding of how algorithms are analyzed. As you saw it is a very mathematical process. If you want to make sure that you understood everything, go back and read the whole chapter again. Maybe also watch my tutorials on YouTube or use Google to find additional examples with solutions. The next chapters will focus more on logic but mathematics will always be a part of them as well. If you are not interested in the mathematical details, feel free to just skip them.

4 – Sorting Algorithms

Oftentimes in programming, we will want to sort values of collections based on certain criteria. We might need to sort a list of numbers, before we apply a specific set of instructions onto it. In such a case, we would write one line of pseudocode, which indicates that we are sorting the list. But what would the runtime complexity of this line be? How efficient is sorting? Well, it depends on the algorithm we use to do it. If we don't specify any particular algorithm, we just assume the most efficient runtime complexity known, which is pseudo-linear (n log n). In this chapter we will take a look at some of the major sorting algorithms, how they work and how efficient they are.

Greedy Algorithms

Before we start talking about the individual algorithms, we will briefly discuss two big categories of algorithms. The first one are the so-called *greedy algorithms.* The main characteristic here is that they always make the choice that seems to be the best at the present moment.

Let's look at a quick example that is not related to sorting. Imagine you have different types of coins, for example 1 cent, 5 cents, 10 cents, 20 cents and 25 cents. You don't just have one per type but an unlimited amount of each. Now I ask you to hand me a certain amount of cents and your job is to do that, using the smallest possible amount of coins. For example if I say give me 25 cents, you could give me a 5 cent coin and two 10 cent coins, but the optimal solution would be one 25 cent coin.

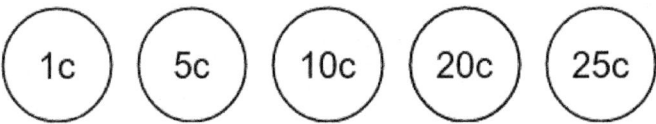

Fig. 4.1: Coin example

A greedy algorithm for this problem would choose the largest coin possible that still fits into the remaining amount, until the desired total value is reached. Let's look at how this could become a problem. If I ask you to hand me 40 cents, what would the greedy algorithm do? It would see that the largest possible coin is 25, since it is less than 40 and pick it. This would leave us with 15 cents remaining. Therefore we pick 10 cents and 5 cents and end up with three coins. However, if you look at the coins, you can see that there is a more efficient solution, which is using two 20 cents coins. As you can see, greedy algorithms don't necessarily always produce the optimal results, even though there are problems, for which they do.

Now all of this isn't really related to sorting algorithms but we will encounter greedy algorithms multiple times throughout this book and since we are going to define a second category (which is related to sorting) next, it is better to have heard of both.

Divide-And-Conquer Algorithms

The second category of algorithms is that of divide-and-conquer algorithms. These are very common in computer science and especially useful when it comes to sorting. What they essentially do is splitting the problem instance up into smaller problems, splitting these up recursively again and again, until the problem size is so small that the solution is almost trivial. These sub-solutions are then combined into a full solution to the initial problem.

The most efficient sorting algorithms like merge sort and quick sort are divide-and-conquer algorithms. We will talk about these in detail throughout this chapter and see what divide-and-conquer does in action there.

Bubble Sort

Before we get to the efficient sorting algorithms however, we will discuss some basic and easy to understand algorithms first. For the start we will look at the so-called *bubble sort*, which is oftentimes used as an introductory example.

Essentially, the bubble sort algorithm always compares two adjacent (means neighboring) elements and swaps them if they are not in the right order. It does this over and over again until the whole list is sorted. Let's look at a simple example.

| 4 | 3 | 2 | 7 | 1 | 6 | 5 |

We start by comparing the first two numbers of this list and see that four is actually larger than three. Since we are sorting in ascending order, we need to swap these two values.

| 3 | 4 | 2 | 7 | 1 | 6 | 5 |

Independently of whether we did perform a swap or not, we now compare the numbers at position two and three. Four is larger than two, so we swap those numbers as well. We now repeat the same process, for the remaining positions and end up with the following list:

| 3 | 2 | 4 | 1 | 6 | 5 | 7 |

As you can see, the list is not yet sorted after one iteration. So how many times do we need to repeat the process until the list is fully sorted? It is easy to notice that after each iteration, at least one more element will be at its correct position. This is because the largest element, which is not yet on its correct position, will inevitably end up there. So in the worst case, we would need to repeat this process n times, while processing one element less in every iteration.

Before this gets too confusing, let us look at the pseudocode for this algorithm:

```
function bubble_sort(list):

    for i := 0 to size(list):
        for j := 0 to size(list) - i - 1:
            if list[j] > list[j+1]:
                swap list[j] and list[j+1]
```

This is basically the code version of the explanation just given. We can now go ahead and analyze it for its worst-case runtime complexity.

```
for i := 0 to size(list):   (n times)
    for j := 0 to size(list) - i - 1: (n-i
times)
        if list[j] > list[j+1]: (1 PO)
            swap list[j] and list[j+1] (1 PO)
```

We can easily see that the first loop runs n times and the second loop runs $n - i$ times, where i is the control variable of the first loop. Mathematically this means that we can use the following formula to determine the amount of primitive operations:

$$2 * \sum_{i=1}^{n} (n - i) = n * (n - 1)$$

If we now multiply this out, we get an expression that tells us pretty clearly what runtime complexity we are dealing with.

$$n * (n - 1) = n^2 - n \rightarrow \quad \theta(n^2)$$

So bubble sort has a quadratic runtime complexity and is thus way less efficient than the algorithms that sort a list in pseudo-linear time. Again, if you are not interested in those detailed mathematical analyses of the algorithms, just skip them. It is enough to know that bubble sort has a quadratic runtime complexity.

SELECTION SORT

In the first chapter, we already briefly mentioned the selection sort algorithm. It essentially looks for the smallest element in a list and swaps it with the element at the first position. Then it repeats the same process for the rest of the list, finds the second smallest element and swaps it with the element at the second position. When we do this n times, the list is definitely sorted. We talked about the process in the first chapter, so let us get directly into the pseudocode.

```
function selection_sort(list):

    for i := 0 to size(list):
        min_value = list[i]
        min_index = i
        for j := i to size(list):
            if list[i] < min_value:
                min_value = list[j]
                min_index = j
        swap list[i] and list[min_index]
```

You can see that we have two loops similar to those of the bubble sort algorithm. Additionally we have two helper variables for storing information about minimum values. Since these are just constant factors, they should not change the runtime complexity. Therefore, we can assume that the runtime complexity will also be quadratic for this algorithm. Let's see if this is the case.

```
for i := 0 to size(list): (n times)
    min_value = list[i] (1 PO)
    min_index = i (1 PO)
    for j := i to size(list): (n-i times)
        if list[i] < min_value: (1 PO)
            min_value = list[j] (1 PO)
            min_index = j (1 PO)
    swap list[i] and list[min_index] (1 PO)
```

So the worst-case formula for the amount of primitive operations would be the following:

$$3n + 3 * \sum_{i=0}^{n} (n - i) = 3n + \frac{3n * (n + 1)}{2}$$

Multiplied out it looks like this:

$$3n + \frac{3n * (n + 1)}{2} = 3n + \frac{3n^2 + 3n}{2} \rightarrow \theta(n^2)$$

So indeed the selection sort also has a quadratic runtime complexity. Therefore it is also inefficient compared to the divide-and-conquer algorithms we are going to learn about.

INSERTION SORT

The last of the simple sorting algorithms we will look at is the insertion sort. The basic idea here is to split the list into a sorted and into an unsorted section. I will explain this algorithm using a basic example.

| 7 | 8 | 5 | 2 | 4 | 6 | 3 |

In the beginning we just pick the first element and say it is sorted. So the seven is the sorted section and every element to the right belongs to the unsorted section. Now in the next step we look at the first unsorted element and determine where it belongs in the sorted list. Since the eight is larger than the seven, we can leave it there and shift the marker for the sorted section by one.

| 7 | 8 | 5 | 2 | 4 | 6 | 3 |

Now we repeat the same process for the next element. Since five is less than seven and eight, it will be placed at the first position of the sorted section.

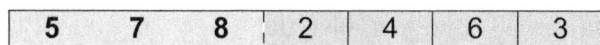

| 5 | 7 | 8 | 2 | 4 | 6 | 3 |

When we do this for all elements, we end up with a fully sorted list.

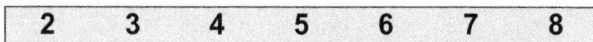

| 2 | 3 | 4 | 5 | 6 | 7 | 8 |

If we look at this superficially, this might feel like it's more efficient than bubble sort or selection sort. It may seem like running through the list n times is enough to sort it. And in a sense it is, but every time we want to determine where an element belongs in the sorted section, we need to compare it with the elements inside of that section. Thus the amount of primitive operations for this depends on n. So we can again assume quadratic time. Let's look at the pseudocode.

```
function selection_sort(list):

    for i := 1 to size(list):
        value := list[i]
        j := i
        while j > 0 and list[j-1] > value:
            list[j] = list[j-1]
            j = j - 1
        list[j] = value
```

Analyzing this algorithm might be a bit confusing, since we are now dealing with a while loop. However, this actually doesn't change too much. Since, we are looking at the worst-case, we can ignore the second condition of this loop and what remains is just the value *j* which gets decremented in each iteration. And essentially *j* is nothing else but *i*.

```
for i := 1 to size(list): (n-1 times)
    value := list[i] (1 PO)
    j := i (1 PO)
    while j > 0 and list[j-1] > value: (i times)
        list[j] = list[j-1] (1 PO)
        j = j - 1 (1 PO)
    list[j] = value (1 PO)
```

Looking at this pseudocode, we can use the following mathematical formula for the runtime complexity:

$$3(n-1) + 2 * \sum_{i=1}^{n-1} i = 3n - 3 + n * (n-1)$$

This can again be rewritten like this:

$$3n - 3 + n * (n-1) = n^2 + 2n - 3 \rightarrow \theta(n^2)$$

So as you can see, even though this algorithm seemed to have a different runtime complexity on a superficial level and had a slightly different code, it still runs in quadratic runtime. However, this algorithm is actually used in combination with divide-and-conquer algorithms in special scenarios. The so-called *Timsort* for example, which is used by Python, combines merge sort and insertion sort.

MERGE SORT

Now we are finally getting to the "efficient" sorting algorithms – the divide-and-conquer algorithms. The first one we are going to look at is the so-called *merge sort*, which we referred to a couple of times in this book already. As the name suggests, it splits the list into sub-lists over and over again, sorts these and then *merges* the sub-solutions into a fully-sorted list. Let's look at a simple example.

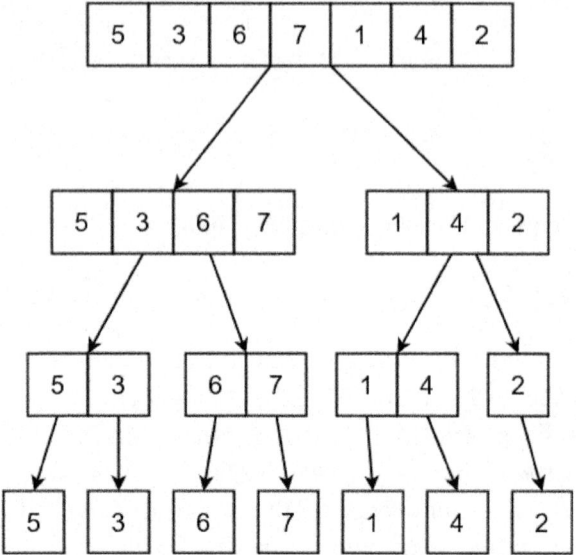

Fig. 4.2: Merge sort dividing

What you can see in the figure above is the first part of the process, namely the division. We start out with an unsorted list and split it up recursively afterwards. We do this until we only have single elements to process. Then we can start merging.

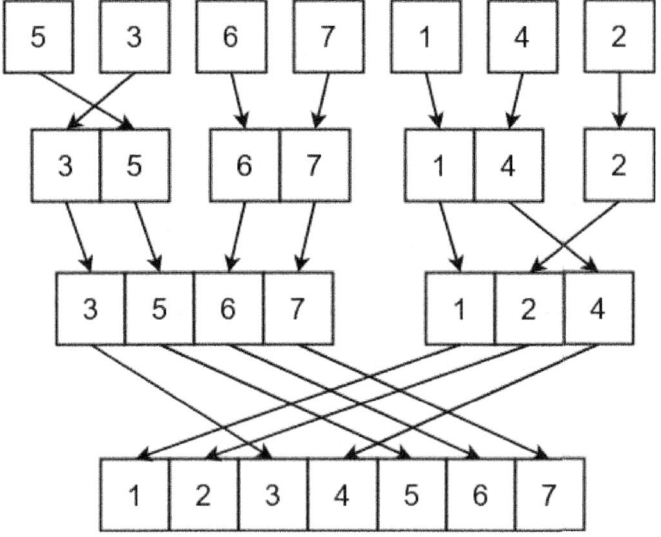

Fig. 4.3: Merge sort merging

The process of merging is actually quite simple. Since all the sub-lists (in the beginning those of length one) are already sorted, all we need to do is to compare the smallest element of the one list to the smallest element of the other list and pick the smaller one. When we have the two sub-lists 3-5-6-7 and 1-2-4 for example, all we need to do is to compare one and three, since the two lists are sorted and there cannot be any smaller numbers. After we have chosen one, we continue by comparing two and three, then four and three and so on, until we end up with a larger combined sorted list.

So in a nutshell it is just splitting up a large list into its individual elements and then combining them into a sorted list step-by-step afterwards. Even though it is pretty easy to understand, the code for this algorithm is quite extensive and analyzing it would be unnecessarily time-consuming. Furthermore, since the main focus of this book is not to constantly analyze algorithms (we did quite a lot of this already), we will determine the runtime complexity of this algorithm, using logical thinking and intuition.

Essentially merge sort can be summarized in three steps:

1. Dividing the given list into sub-lists
2. Recursive call for sorting
3. Merging the results

Dividing the list can be done in constant time, so we can ignore this step for now. Merging the results is done in linear time, since we need to merge n elements. So because of step three, we already have at least linear time. But now the question is: How many times do we need to merge? For this we can look at step two. We are halving the problem size with each recursion. When you look at Fig. 4.2 again, you can see that we have n individual elements to merge. Merging happens in linear time and we need to merge n times. However, the problem size is one, which means that we need n operations for the first level of merging (ignoring constants). After that, we have four sorted sub-lists, which means we need to merge four times. But again the problem size is not n. It is n divided by four (except for the single element on the right). So roughly speaking we need to merge four times and the problem size is n divided by four.

Thus we have *n* operations at this level as well. After that we end up with two sub-lists that are sorted. This again means that we need to merge two lists that are half the size of *n*. The factor two disappears and we have *n* operations once more.

So essentially, we had three times *n* operations in this example. The amount of operations depends on how many levels of splitting and merging we have. And since we are halving our list with each recursion, the amount of levels is the logarithm (base two) of the list size. In order to understand why this is the case, ask the following question: How many times do I need to divide the problem size by two (splitting) in order to end up with individual elements (or lists of size one). The answer is the logarithm base two of the problem size.

$$levels = \theta(\log_2 n) \rightarrow \theta(n \log n)$$

In a nutshell, we have to perform a linear amount of operations at each level and the amount of levels is logarithmic. Therefore the runtime complexity of merge sort is pseudo-linear. An interesting fact here is that the worst-case complexity of merge sort is the same as the average-case and the best-case complexity. This is because the process is always the same. We cannot have more or less than a linear amount of comparisons while merging and we cannot have more or less than a logarithmic amount of levels. Even if we apply the algorithm onto an already sorted list, it will split and merge and produce the same runtime complexity.

QUICK SORT

When you ask Google which sorting algorithm is the best one, most pages will tell you that it's *quick sort*. Even though there might be some better choices (like combinations of sorting algorithms), this is true for the most part. Quick sort is another divide-and-conquer algorithm that is super-efficient and even though it has the same average-case runtime complexity (not worst-case) as merge sort, it is usually considered more efficient because its constant factors are smaller. Let's look at how it works.

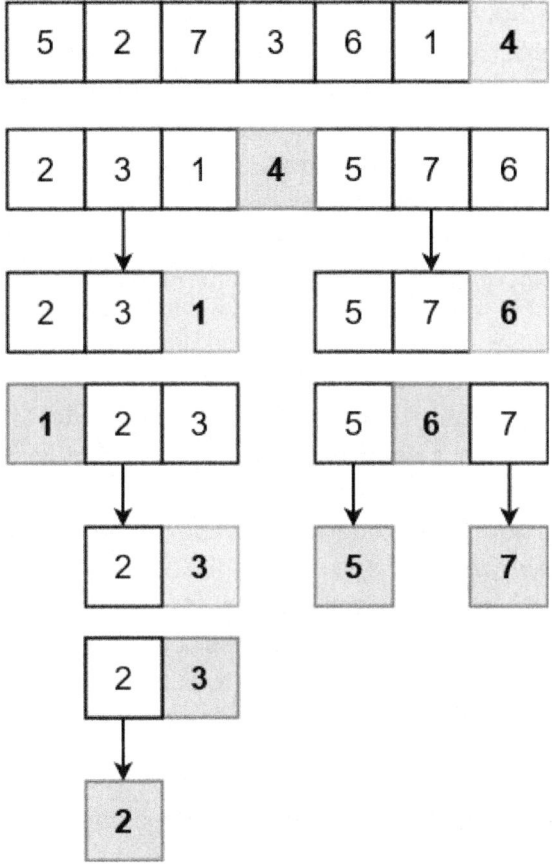

Fig. 4.4: Quick sort

The quick sort algorithm uses a so-called pivot element in order to sort the list. We can freely define which element shall be chosen for this. In the figure above, we decided to always choose the last element of the list. We could also go ahead and choose the first one or the one in the middle. However, after choosing this pivot element, we go through the whole list and put all the smaller elements to its left and all the larger elements to its right. Notice that the order of these elements among themselves does not change. This means that the sorting algorithm is *stable*. When we have done that, we have found the correct place for our pivot element. After that we split the list into two and repeat the same process until we get the correct position for all elements.

It is easy to see why this algorithm has a pseudo-linear average-case runtime complexity. We basically reposition the elements in linear time and we do this as many times as there are levels. Usually this will be logarithmic. However, the worst-case complexity of this algorithm is quadratic. Even though it is very unlikely, we could encounter a list that is structured in such a way, that after every split, the pivot element ends up at the last or first position. The amount of levels would then be linear, which means that we would end up with a quadratic complexity.

Nevertheless quicksort is considered to be the most efficient sorting algorithm (excluding combined algorithms or non-comparison-based algorithms), since the quadratic complexity almost never happens in reality. Compared to merge sort, most of the time, quick sort is just faster and needs fewer operations.

Now there are countless other sorting algorithms out there that we haven't talked about. Some are radix sort, counting sort, comb sort and Tim sort. It would just be too much to cover all of them. However, you should now have a decent understanding of sorting algorithms and runtime complexity. So if you are interested in other algorithms as well, just go ahead and look them up online. If you want to know how sorting is done in Python for example, take a look at Tim sort. It is a combination of quick sort and insertion sort, which prevents the quadratic scenario of the former by switching to the latter.

5 – Graph Theory & Algorithms

Now we get to a whole different topic. Even though this is not a math textbook, we will briefly cover some graph theory here, since this field is crucial for algorithms and data structures. We are not going to talk too much about various properties and definitions of graphs here. Our main focus will be on applying algorithms onto graphs and analyzing their complexity.

Graph Theory Basics

Let's start with the most basic question of what a graph actually is. Fundamentally it is just a data structure consisting of vertices and edges.

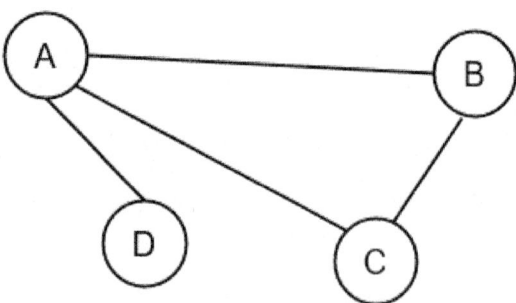

Fig. 5.1: Basic undirected graph

A graph can be directed or undirected. In a directed graph, the edges have directions, which means that being able to go from A to B doesn't imply being able to go from B to A. If a graph doesn't have any circles or cycles, we call it a tree.

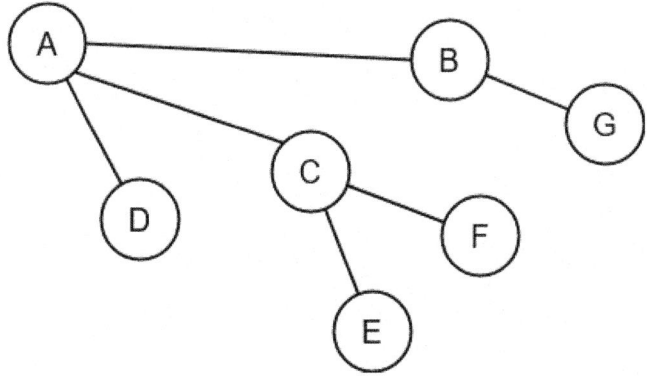

Fig. 5.2: Basic tree

Now there are a lot of additional labels and properties such a graph can have. As I said, we are going to skip these unless they are relevant for the algorithm we are discussing. In such a case, we will explain them on the fly.

BREADTH FIRST SEARCH

So let us get into the first algorithm. Let's say we have a starting vertex A and we want to examine all vertices that can be reached from it. A practical use case of this could be to check if there is a path from A to any other particular vertex. Or to find out how many edges the shortest path between two vertices has. One way to do this is using the so-called *breadth first search*, oftentimes abbreviated *BFS*.

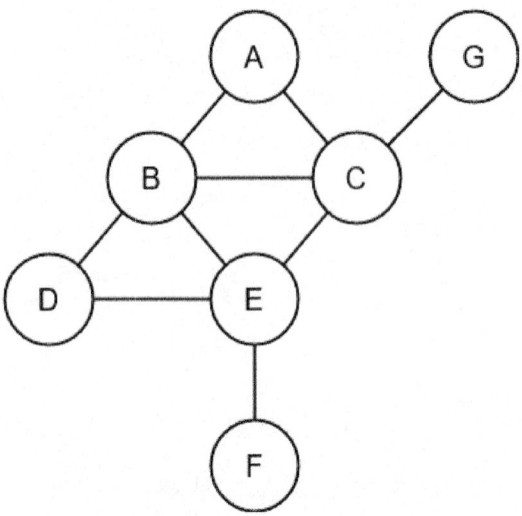

Fig. 5.3: Sample graph for BFS

Roughly speaking in the BFS, we prefer breadth over depth. This means that we are first going to look at all the neighbors of our starting vertex before continuing to go deeper into the graph. Then we are going to look at all the neighbors of the neighbors and so on.

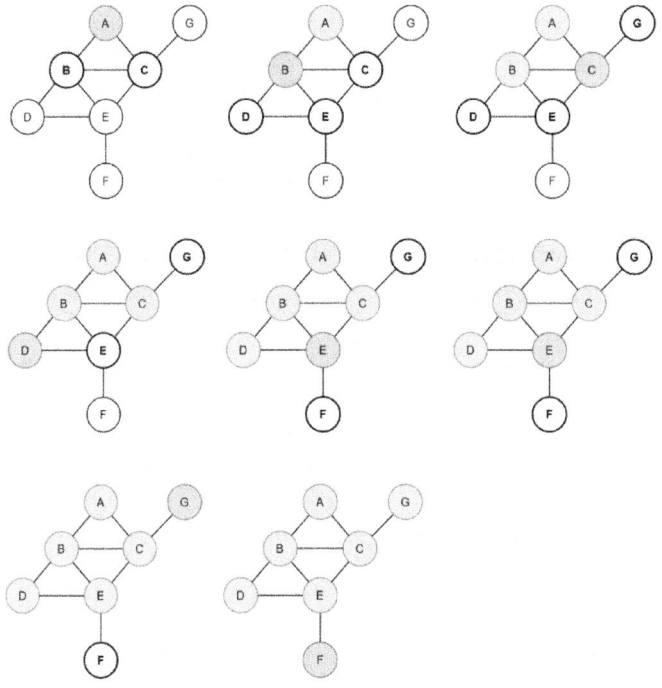

Fig. 5.4: BFS algorithm

In the figure above, you can see the order of discovery. First we cover all neighbors of A. Then we detect all the neighbors of the neighbors. Only after that, we consider the neighbors of level three (which is only F).

We are not going to analyze the exact algorithm in detail. But the runtime complexity is the following:

$$O(V + E)$$

The algorithmic complexity of BFS depends on the sum of the amount of vertices and the amount of edges. Since the amount of edges can vary from $O(1)$ to $O(V^2)$, we cannot really specify a runtime complexity here other than V + E.

DEPTH FIRST SEARCH

The alternative to the breadth first search (BFS) is the *depth first search (DFS)*. As the name already suggests, the idea is the opposite from the BFS. Before we consider any additional neighbors of the starting point, we want to go as far into the graph as possible. Let's see what a DFS would look like in a slightly different graph than the one we used before.

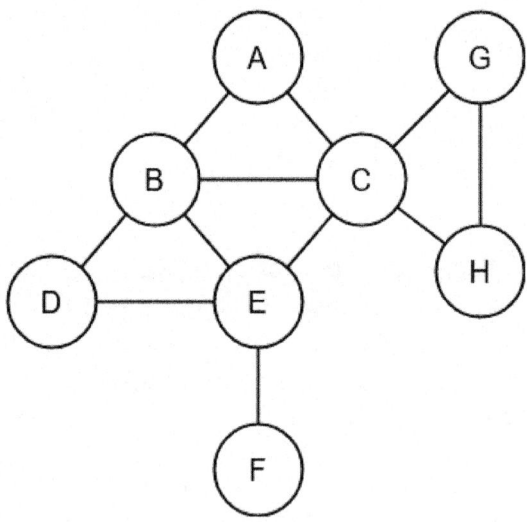

Fig. 5.5: Sample graph for DFS

As you can see it is essentially the same graph with one additional vertex H and two additional edges to C and G. We add these components in order to see how DFS works more clearly.

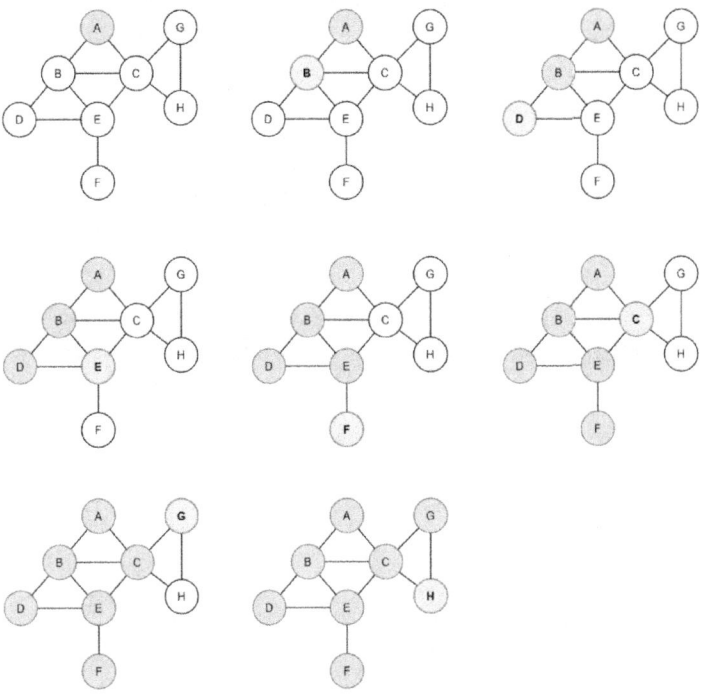

Fig. 5.6: DFS algorithm

In the illustration above, you can see one possible scenario of a DFS. You can clearly see that the algorithm only goes to neighbors of the initial vertex if there are no other vertices available.

$$O(V + E)$$

The runtime complexity of the DFS is the same as that of the BFS. However there are some differences. For example the BFS uses the *Queue* data structure in its algorithm, whereas the DFS uses the *Stack* data structure (more about those in the next chapter). Depending on what problem you are trying to solve, you need to think about which traversal approach might be more appropriate.

DIJKSTRA ALGORITHM

Now let us talk a little bit about finding the shortest path from a vertex A to a vertex B. With a BFS we can find such a path but only if all edges are equally good or bad. When we have weighted edges things get more difficult.

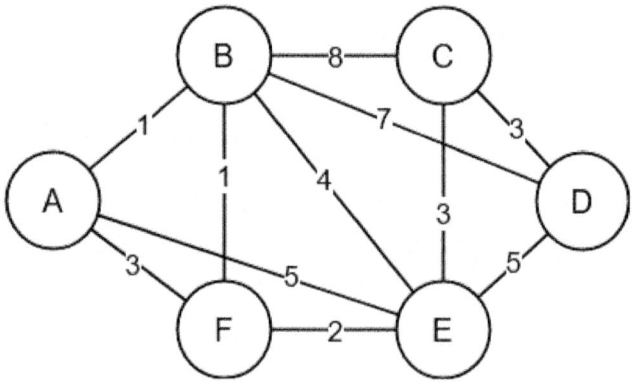

Fig. 5.7: Weighted graph

Using a simple BFS to find the shortest path from A to any other vertex is not going to work. For example look at the path from A to F. Using the direct connection has a cost of three, whereas going from A to B and then to F has a cost of two. More edges but less cost. A BFS is not able to recognize that.

Therefore we need to use another algorithm called *Dijkstra.* Again, we will mainly focus on the way it works instead of dissecting every line of its pseudocode.

What we basically do is picking a starting point and then writing down how much it costs to reach each vertex using a single step. Then we choose the node with the smallest cost and write down the previous vertex, we accessed it from.

Steps	A	B	C	D	E	F	Choice	Prev
1	-	1	∞	∞	5	3	B	A

With one step, we can reach B with a cost of one, E with a cost of 5 and F with a cost of three. The cost of all the other nodes is infinite, since we cannot reach them at all. So we choose B and note that we accessed B from A.

Steps	A	B	C	D	E	F	Choice	Prev
1	-	1	∞	∞	5	3	B	A
2			9	8	5	2	F	B

Since we chose B, we now look at all the vertices we can access within one step from B. All nodes can be accessed, so we write down the cost for each of them. Notice however, that we need to add the cost of one that we still have for going from A to B. For example the vertex C has a cost of nine, because it costs one to go from A to B and eight to go from B to C. When we are done with writing down all values, we can see that the cost for F is the smallest. So we choose F and write down that we got there from B. This is important because going directly to F is more expensive. The cost of E doesn't change, since it is the same.

Steps	A	B	C	D	E	F	Choice	Prev
1	-	1	∞	∞	5	3	B	A
2			9	8	5	2	F	B
3			9	8	4		E	F

We are now looking at all the neighbors of F. These neighbors are B and E. Since B is irrelevant, we only care about E. Accessing E from F instead of A or B is in fact more efficient, since it costs one unit less. C and D cannot be accessed from F, so we don't change these values. The cost is smallest for E, so we choose it and note F as the previous vertex.

Steps	A	B	C	D	E	F	Choice	Prev
1	-	1	∞	∞	5	3	B	A
2			9	8	5	2	F	B
3			9	8	4		E	F
4			7	8			C	E

The same process is repeated and we see that C is the newest cheapest vertex we can get to. Using E to access C saves us two cost units. This is not the case for D. Going through E to reach D is actually more expensive.

Steps	A	B	C	D	E	F	Choice	Prev
1	-	1	∞	∞	5	3	B	A
2			9	8	5	2	F	B
3			9	8	4		E	F
4			7	8			C	E
5				8			D	B

Then of course the last vertex is D but we need to keep in mind where we accessed D from. The cost of this node is the same for a couple of iterations already. It was first discovered from the vertex B and has never gotten cheaper ever since. Therefore, we can write down B as its discoverer or previous node. With all that information we can now go ahead and draw a new graph, which shows us all the shortest paths from the starting point A.

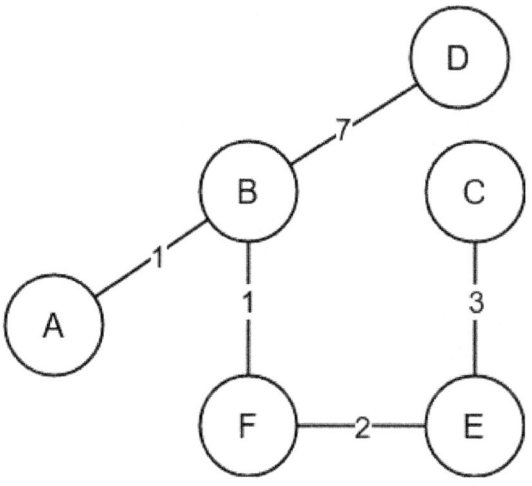

Fig. 5.8: Distance graph

As you can see, wherever you want to go from the starting point A, you only have a single path and this path is the most efficient path.

Now even though we are not going to look at the exact implementations of Dijkstra's algorithm, we will briefly talk about its runtime complexity. If we were to just naively go ahead and implement this algorithm in a simple way, we would end up with a quadratic runtime complexity.

$$O(V^2)$$

However there are implementations of this algorithm using the *priority queue* data structure, which allow the following runtime complexity:

$$O([V + E] * \log V)$$

If you are interested in a deeper analysis of these variations, just go online, look for the pseudocode for Dijkstra's algorithm and apply the techniques used in the previous chapters.

KRUSKAL ALGORITHM

Last but not least for this chapter, we will learn how to find *minimum* and *maximum spanning trees* in graphs. In other words: We will learn how to find a sub-graph that still allows us to access all vertices but using a minimum amount of edges with either a minimum or a maximum weight.

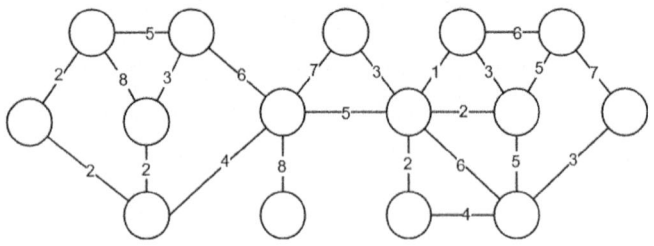

Fig. 5.9: Sample graph for Kruskal

Let's look at the graph above and try to find the minimum spanning tree. Don't get confused by the large amount of vertices and edges. The algorithm we are going to look at is extremely simple and thus we choose a graph that is a bit larger.

So how can we go about this? We want to end up with a graph that has as many edges as necessary to still connect all vertices but at the same time a minimal total cost. Here the so-called *Kruskal* algorithm comes into play. It is very simple and every elementary school kid would probably understand it. All we need to do is to mark all edges with the lowest cost and not create any circles.

Essentially this means just marking all the edges with weight one and two, as long as we don't create any circles by doing that. Then do the same thing for three, four and so on until all vertices are covered.

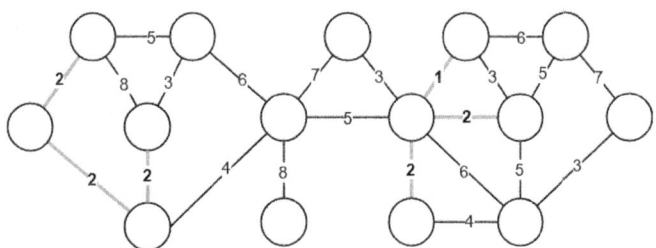

Fig. 5.10: First two iterations of Kruskal

After marking all edges with weight one and two, we have covered around half of the vertices. We now continue to do the same thing with the higher weights.

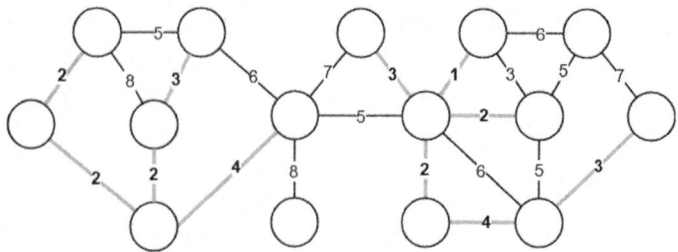

Fig. 5.11: First four iterations of Kruskal

Notice that one edge with weight three was skipped here, since it would create a circle and thus add no value to our spanning tree. When we go on with this process until all nodes are covered, we end up with the following spanning tree.

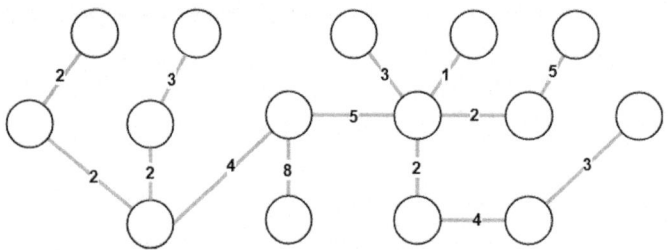

Fig. 5.12: Minimum spanning tree

The same procedure can be done the other way around (starting with the largest weights) to find the maximum spanning tree. The runtime complexity of the Kruskal algorithm is pseudo-linear and depending on the amount of edges.

$$O(E * \log(E))$$

Again, if you want a detailed analysis of the algorithm, look it up online. We don't want every chapter in this book to look like chapter three and four. Therefore, for less important algorithms, we focus more on the intuition instead of the full pseudocode.

After reading this chapter you should now have a decent understanding of what graphs are and also about four major algorithms that are crucial in this field. In the next chapter we will finally get into the details of the second big topic of this book, namely data structures.

6 – Data Structures

Up until now we mainly talked about algorithms, runtime complexity and how to solve certain problems like sorting or finding a minimum spanning tree. While doing that, we mentioned at some point that there are certain algorithms for certain problems that make use of data structures like priority queues for example. The usage of these data structures allows for a more efficient algorithm. And even though we mentioned some data structures like linked lists superficially, we never took the time to cover the individual data structures in detail. This is what we are going to do in this chapter. We will get an overview of the most important data structures there are and we will analyze the runtime complexity of their operations like accessing elements, removing elements etc.

Linked List

Since we already briefly covered its workings, let us start with the linked list. We will skip the ordinary array, since it is pretty trivial and the runtime complexities are obvious. If they aren't for you: Everything except for the access (constant time) happens in linear time. That's it about arrays basically. So let us quickly recap what a linked list actually is. I hope you don't judge me for recycling the graph I already used in the second chapter.

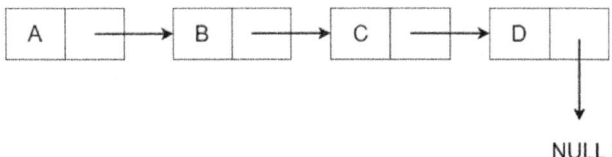

NULL

Fig. 6.1: Structure of a linked list

A linked list is essentially a collection of nodes, which consist of a value and a pointer. The first node is called head and (at least in a singly-linked list) has no other node pointing to it. It is the starting point for all operations. The pointer of this node points to another node, which again has a value and a pointer that points to yet another node and so on. This continues until we get to the last node, which's pointer is pointing to *null*.

ACCESSING ELEMENTS

Because of this structure the linked list is dynamic in its size. We can always just create a new independent node and either let the last node point to it or squeeze it into the list somewhere. The problem with this though is that accessing an element of the list is no longer possible in constant time. We cannot just calculate the address of a position. What we need to do in order to access a position is to go through all the nodes before this position. This leaves us with a linear runtime complexity for accessing elements.

$$O(n)$$

You might be wondering why I switched to using the Big O notation instead of the theta notation. The reason for that is that the Big O notation indicates the upper boundary. When we are talking about exact mathematical results, we can use the theta notation because it tells us the exact complexity. However, when we just talk about what the worst-case is, the big O notation is certainly sufficient. We don't need an additional lower boundary here.

FINDING ELEMENTS

Finding elements in a linked list is pretty similar to accessing a position. Instead of looking for the index, we now look for a specific value. In the worst case, we have to traverse the whole list. Thus we also have a linear time complexity here.

$$O(n)$$

INSERTING ELEMENTS

When it comes to inserting elements into a linked list, things get a little bit more complex. It depends on what we mean by inserting. If we are given the exact positions (means memory addresses) of where we need to insert our element, the mere act of inserting can be done in constant time. So if we have an iterator for example, inserting is very efficient. If we need to traverse the list to get to the respective position on the other hand, we obviously end up with linear time as well. However, inserting is considered to be possible in constant time, since we can use things like iterators to make things more efficient.

$$O(1) \quad OR \quad O(n)$$

DELETING ELEMENTS

For deleting elements it is the same thing. The act of deletion is very simple and does not depend on the list size. If we have an iterator, which allows us to get to the positions in constant time, we can delete elements in constant time. Otherwise we have to traverse the list and have linear time. So it's the same as with inserting.

$$O(1) \quad OR \quad O(n)$$

All in all, the main benefit of linked lists is their dynamic size. We don't need so specify any fixed amount of slots. We can always add and remove elements and by that increase and decrease the list size. This is a major advantage that this data structure has over arrays for example.

Another thing that is worth mentioning is that, besides singly-linked lists, there are also doubly-linked lists. They have two pointers in each node (instead of just one), which point at the previous and at the next element. The runtime complexities are the same though.

STACK

The *stack* data structure follows the so-called *LIFO* (Last In First Out) or *FILO* (First In Last Out) principle. As the name suggests, we can stack elements on top of each other and then work through them in reverse order.

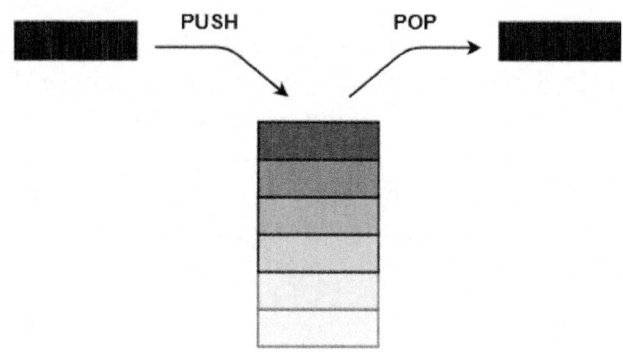

Fig. 6.2: Stack data structure

In a stack we have two basic operations – *push* and *pop*. Pushing an element onto the stack means placing it on top of all the other elements. Popping an element out of the stack means removing the element at the top. You can see why it is called LIFO. The elements that are pushed into the stack *last* are popped out of the stack *first*. There is also an additional operation called *peek*, which allows us to access the element at the top, without removing it.

PUSHING AND POPPING

Obviously pushing an element on top of a stack and removing the element at the top are simple operations that can be done in constant time. It doesn't matter how large the stack is, the runtime remains the same.

$$O(1)$$

FINDING AND ACCESSING

Finding or accessing particular values in a stack is not something that you would usually want to do. In fact stacks are primarily used for things like recursions and function calls (this is where StackOverflows happen oftentimes). So it doesn't really make a lot of sense to look for a particular value inside of a stack. However, if you wanted to do it, you could do it in linear time, since you need to pop all the values that come before the value you are looking for. This is similar to going through all nodes and pointers in a linked list before getting to your target.

$$O(1)$$

QUEUE

Queues are pretty similar to stacks. In a sense, stacks could be described as LIFO queues. The difference is just the order of processing. In queues the elements that enter the data structure first are processed first.

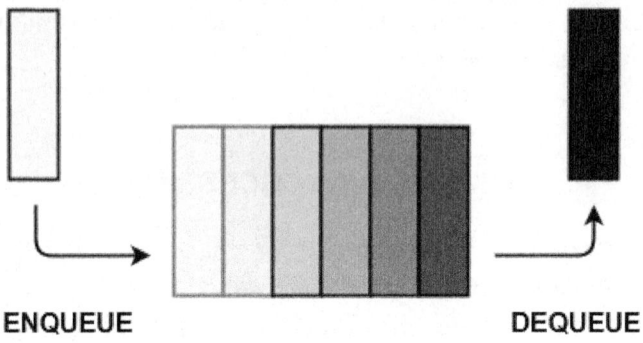

ENQUEUE   **DEQUEUE**

Fig. 6.3: Queue data structure

As you can see in the figure above, a queue looks like a stack flipped on its side. Whatever enters the queue first, will also be processed first. Whatever enters the queue last, will also be processed last. Thus this data structure operates by the *FIFO* or *LILO* principle.

RUNTIME COMPLEXITIES

The runtime complexities for the individual operations are the same as for the stack. Enqueuing is like pushing and dequeuing is like popping. They can be done in constant time. Finding or accessing a specific element can be done in linear time.

PRIORITY QUEUE

One special form of queue is the so-called *priority queue* that we already mentioned briefly when we talked about Dijkstra's algorithm. Essentially it is just a queue, where each element has a certain priority to it. Instead of following the LIFO or the FIFO principle, the order of processing is based on these priorities.

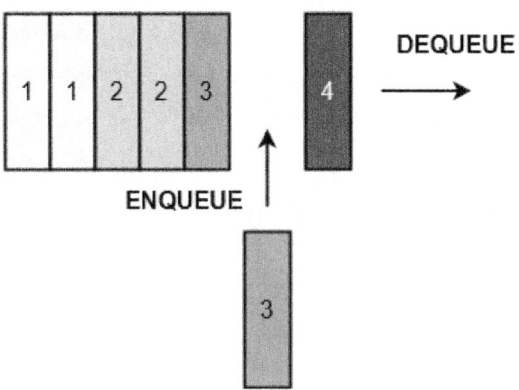

Fig. 6.4: Priority queue data structure

That's the general idea behind priority queues but how can they be implemented efficiently? Sure we could just go ahead and use a sorted linked list to implement it. But then enqueuing and dequeuing could only be done in linear time, since we need to iterate through all nodes that come before our target node. However, there is a way to make enqueuing, dequeuing and finding elements possible in logarithmic time. This can be done using the *heap* data structure as a backbone.

HEAP

A *heap* is essentially just a tree and therefore a graph without circles or cycles. But this tree has a special property, called the *heap property*. Every node in a (binary) heap has a left and a right child (can be null as well, which makes the node a leaf node). The heap property demands that the value of every child is smaller than the value of its parent. This is at least the case in a *max-heap*. In a *min-heap* it is the other way around, which means that every child must have a larger value than its parent node.

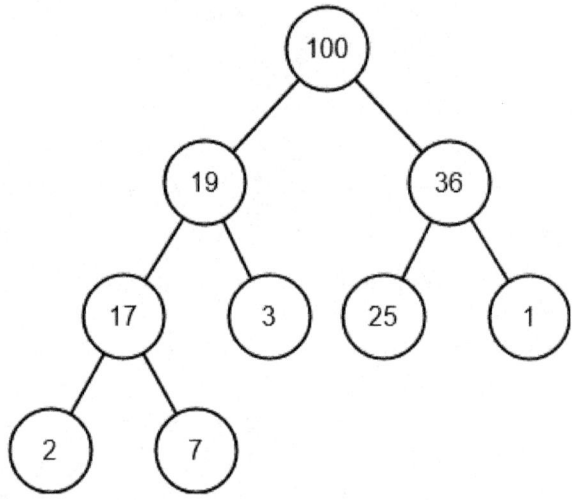

Fig. 6.5: Max-Heap data structure

As you can see, the value 100 is at the root, because it is the highest priority (in a max-heap). All the other elements are smaller.

INSERTING ELEMENTS

Now when we go ahead and insert elements into this data structure, we need to make sure that we maintain the heap property. We can do this by performing an operation called *heapify-up*. First we just append the new element at the next slot available. We fill up the list from left to right.

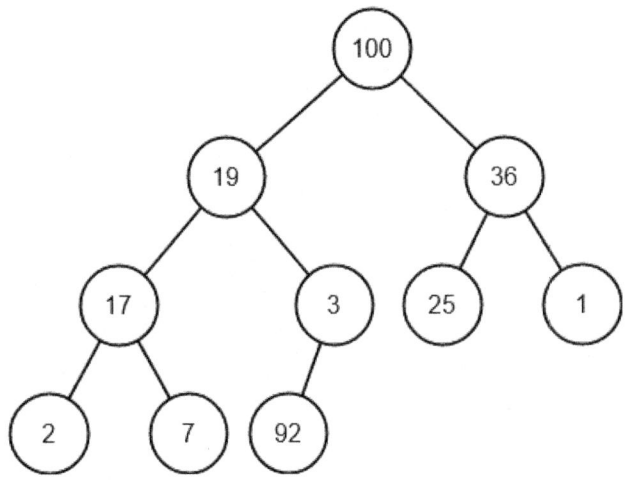

Fig. 6.6: Appending a new element

In the figure above, you can see that we are adding the value 92 to our heap. The first step is to just append it and you can see that this clearly violates the heap property. So the next step is to do a heapify-up. This means that we compare the value of this node to the value of its parent. In this case 92 is larger than 3. Because of that we swap their positions.

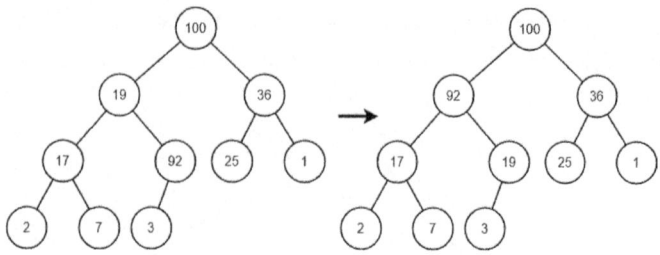

Fig. 6.7: Heapify-up

After that we do another comparison and see that 92 is greater than 19 as well. Now 92 is the parent of 17 and 19. Since it was larger than its own parent, it is automatically also larger than its "sibling". Last but not least we compare it to the root node and see that 92 is less than 100. The heapify-up is completed and our data structure fulfills the heap property again.

Since you have some experience with runtime complexities already, you can probably see that this operation is possible in logarithmic time. Appending an element happens in constant time and the maximum amount of comparisons made by the heapify-up, is the amount of levels in the worst case. We only need to compare an element to its parent. If it is always larger than its parent, it will end up at the root node.

$$O(\log n)$$

Notice that the process is the exact same for min-heaps except for the fact that the smaller values get to the top. This doesn't make any difference in terms of runtime complexity.

DELETING ELEMENTS

By inserting elements into a heap we can enqueue elements and maintain the correct order. But what happens when we want to dequeue an element? In this case we would delete the root node, since it has the highest priority. But then our tree would be broken. The solution for this is the so-called *heapify-down* operation.

When we delete the root node (in order to dequeue and process it for example), we replace it by the last node of the heap. Then we look at its child-nodes and compare it to the largest of them (or smallest in a min-heap). If our element is smaller than its largest child, we swap their positions. We continue this process until the heap property is satisfied again. Let's look at a simple example.

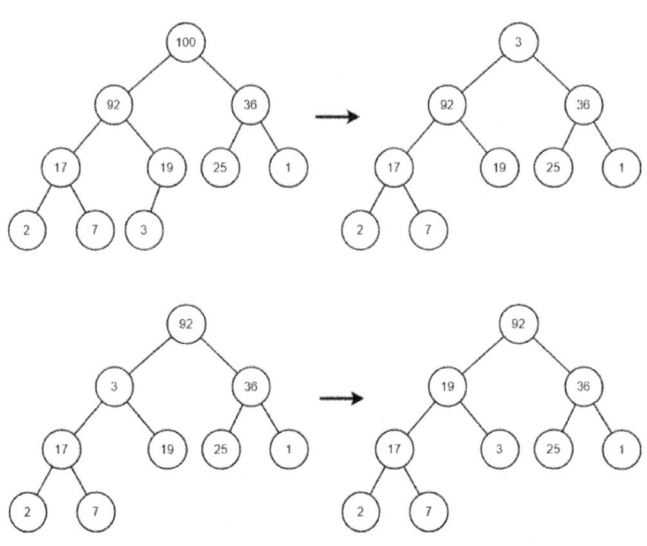

Fig. 6.8: Heapify-down

We use the resulting heap of our previous insertion as an example. First we remove the root node and replace it with the last element. Then we start our heapify-down process by comparing the new root to the largest child, which is 92 in this case. Because 92 is larger than 3, we swap their positions. We repeat the process and end up with the heap that you can see in the figure above. The heap property is satisfied.

The runtime complexity can again be derived easily. We cannot have more comparisons than there are levels and the amount of levels is not more than the logarithm (base) two of the amount of elements. Therefore the runtime complexity is logarithmic again.

$$O(\log n)$$

As you can see the heap data structure allows for an extremely efficient implementation of the priority queue. We can enqueue and dequeue elements based on their priority in logarithmic time.

BINARY SEARCH TREE

Last but not least for this chapter we will talk about the *binary search tree*. As the name already tells us this is also a tree data structure. But its structure is different from that of the heap. In a binary search tree all the elements that are smaller than the root node are part of the left sub-tree and all elements that are larger than the root node are part of the right sub-tree.

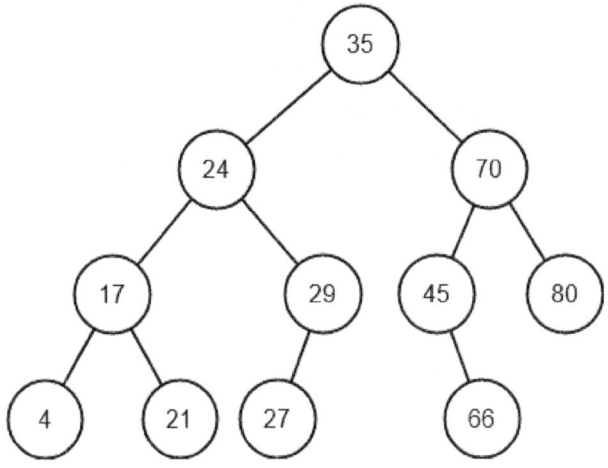

Fig. 6.9: Binary search tree

Notice also that every sub-tree of a binary search tree is a binary search tree itself. When we look at the left sub-tree, you can see that 24 is the root node and all the elements that are smaller are to its left and all the elements that are larger are to its right.

FINDING ELEMENTS

This property can be very beneficial for us, when we try to find values. Think about it: Whenever we want to get to a certain value, we can forget about one complete sub-tree. If the value we are looking for is smaller than the current node, we can completely ignore all the elements to its right. Then we do the same thing in the sub-tree until we get to our desired value. This means that the amount of comparisons we need to do depends on the height of the binary search tree. Does this mean that we can find values in logarithmic time? Not exactly! If we are dealing with a balanced tree, like the one in the figure above, we have logarithmic runtime because we are roughly halving the problem size with each step. However, binary trees are not necessarily balanced.

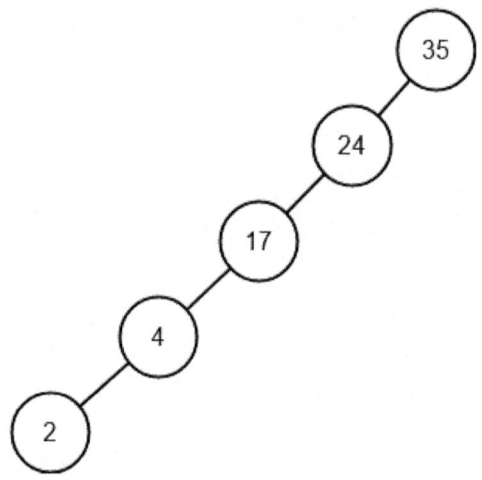

Fig. 6.10: Unfavorable binary search tree

What you see in the figure above is a valid binary search tree. We have a root node, all the smaller values are to its left and all the larger values are to its right. The problem is though that there are no smaller values, since the root is also the maximum. And this is not only true for the tree in general but for each sub-tree as well.

The height of this tree is equal to the amount of elements. In order to get to the value two for example, we need to traverse the whole tree. And because worst cases like this one are still valid binary search trees, we say that finding an element has a linear worst-case runtime complexity. However, it is very unlikely to encounter a list like this one.

$$O(n)$$

INSERTING AND DELETING ELEMENTS

The logic for insertion and deletion is pretty much the same. In order to know where to insert an element or to delete an existing element, we need to navigate to the respective position. The amount of steps necessary to do that depends on its height as we already know. Because of that, these operations also have a linear worst-case complexity.

$$O(n)$$

As you can see, the major problem here is that we cannot assume that binary search trees will always be balanced. If this was the case, we would have a logarithmic runtime complexity for all fundamental operations. Because of that there are more advanced tree data structures that are *self-balancing* and those will be the topic of the next chapter.

7 – SELF-BALANCING TREES

In order to prevent edge cases and unfavorable structures of search trees, computer scientists came up with the idea of self-balancing trees. If we are able to ensure that a search tree will always be balanced, we can ensure that the search can always be done in logarithmic time. In this chapter we will look at three major self-balancing trees and how they work.

AVL TREE

Let us start out with the *AVL tree*, which has its name from its inventors – Adelson-Velski and Landis. The basic idea behind this search tree is a limitation to the height difference of the sub-trees of each node. When we notice that one side of the tree (or sub-tree) has too many levels compared to the other side, we don't accept this and rebalance the tree.

In order to implement this, we assign a so-called *balance factor* to each node. This balance factor is calculated by subtracting the height of the left sub-tree from the height of the right sub-tree. If both sides have the same height, we will get a zero. If the right side has a larger height than the left one, we will get a positive number and otherwise we will get a negative number. For a balanced node we demand a balance factor of either -1, 0 or 1.

$$balance\,factor = height(right) - height(left)$$

$$balance\,factor \in \{-1,0,1\} \quad \rightarrow \quad balanced$$

This essentially means that we only accept a maximum height difference of one until we consider a node (or sub-tree) to be unbalanced.

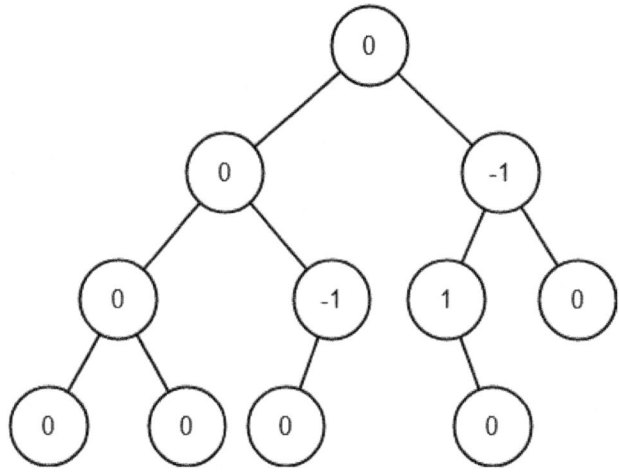

Fig. 7.1: Balanced AVL tree with balance factors

The tree above is an example of a balanced AVL tree. Don't mistake the balance factors for values though. This notation is not 100% correct. Usually you would put the values inside of the nodes and the balance factors beside them. However, you can see that this tree is pretty balanced. There is no sub-tree in it that has a height difference larger than one.

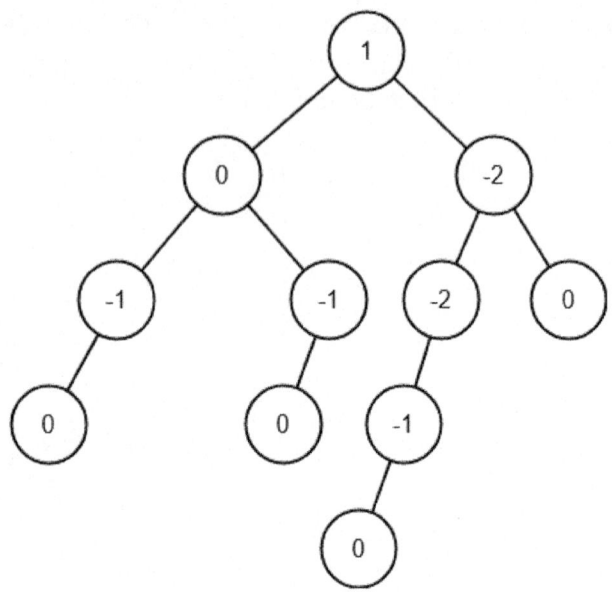

Fig. 7.2: Unbalanced AVL tree

Here on the other hand you can see an unbalanced example. Notice though that the root node is not unbalanced. The height of the left sub-tree is three and the height of the right one is four. That is an acceptable difference. But when you look at the right sub-tree you can see that we have two unbalanced nodes there. Therefore we now know that just looking at the balance factor of the root node is not enough for determining if a tree is balanced or not. The root node can be perfectly balanced and we can still have height differences of a hundred inside of our sub-trees.

Let's think about it. When do we actually need to check if our tree is still balanced? When we search for certain values, we need the tree to be balanced (for logarithmic time), but if it was balanced the last time, it will also be balanced this time. We can only make a tree unbalanced by inserting or deleting elements. Thus we need to make sure that our tree is still balanced after those critical operations and rebalance it if it is not.

We already talked about the insertion and deletion in a binary search tree. These operations are possible in logarithmic time (when balanced) and they remain the same for AVL trees. The only thing that we need to add is the rebalancing and for this we have four possible cases.

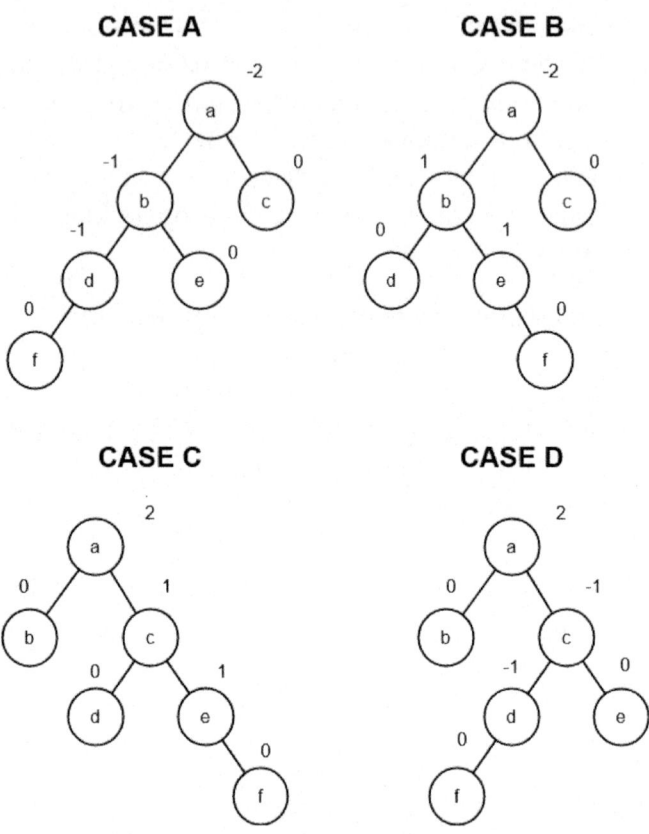

Fig. 7.3: Four cases for rebalancing

These are the four fundamental cases in which we need to rebalance. Depending on where the imbalances are and what the sub-trees look like, we need to perform different operations.

In case A and B the tree is unbalanced to the left. However in case A the root node of the left sub-tree has a balance factor of negative one (or zero) and in case B of positive one. That actually makes a difference. In the first case we can rebalance the tree by performing a simple right rotation at the root node. This means that the node *b* becomes the root node and the node *a* becomes the right child of *b*. At the same time the right child of *b* becomes the left child of *a*.

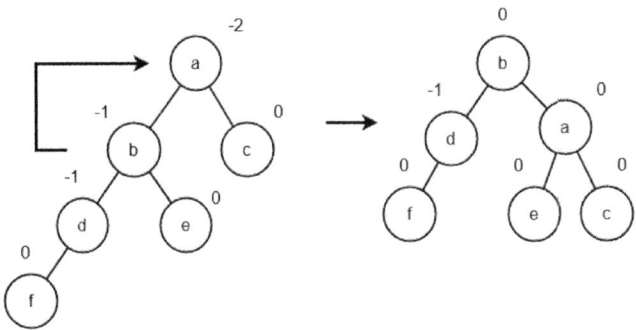

Fig. 7.4: Single right rotation for case A

The rebalancing for case B looks different. In case A the right child of *b* becomes the left child of *a*. But if this child has child-nodes itself, things get problematic. We would then end up with an unbalanced tree. So what we do instead is transforming case B to case A with a single left rotation at node *b*. After that, a right rotation at the root node follows. This is a so-called *left-right rotation* and applied onto case B it results in a balanced tree.

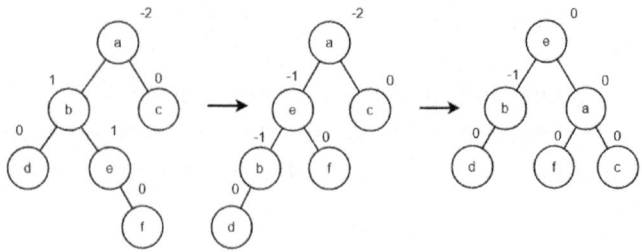

Fig. 7.5: Double left-right rotation for case B

You can see that after the first left rotation we end up with a tree that fits into case A. Then, all we need to do is to perform a single right rotation.

The cases C and D are the exact same as A and B but just from right to left. So in case C the rebalancing is done by a single left rotation. Here the left child of node c becomes the right child of node a. In the same way, we need to perform a double right-left rotation in case D.

These four cases are all types of imbalances that we can encounter. However they might not only occur at the root node but at every node in the search tree. Whenever we add or remove an element, we work our way up from the bottom. We fix local imbalances first. Once a sub-tree is balanced we start looking at its parent node.

The rotations themselves can be done in constant time and there are never more rotations than levels in our tree. Therefore we have a logarithmic worst-case runtime complexity for inserting, deleting and finding elements in AVL trees.

$$O(\log n)$$

B-Tree

The search trees that we have looked at up until now are pretty decent when our data is in the RAM and can be accessed very fast. When we get to really big sets of data however, we will usually make use of hard drives or other external storage media. Accessing data on a hard drive takes much more time than accessing data in the RAM. Therefore, when we want to process data from an external storage medium, we navigate to the respective addresses and load the relevant part of the data into the RAM.

External storage media usually have a block-oriented structure and whenever we access some data we access the full block. Thus it makes sense to combine multiple nodes in order to flatten our tree and minimize the amount of accesses. We already saw that the runtime complexity of inserting, deleting and finding depends on the tree height. So if we find a way to decrease the height, we can also decrease the amount of memory accesses.

All this can be done using a so-called *B-Tree,* which is a self-balancing tree, in which multiple nodes are combined into one block. The idea here is to let the tree grow more in terms of width than in terms of height. Let us look at the formal definition of a B-Tree.

Definition of a B-Tree of order *m*:

1. All leaf-nodes are at the same level
2. Each node can have a maximum of *m* child-nodes
3. Each inner node (means not a leaf-node) has a minimum of [m/2] child-nodes. The root node has a minimum of two child-nodes.
4. Each node has one more child-nodes than it has keys

As always, I am not claiming that this definition is 100% complete. But it is definitely enough in order to understand the concept of B-Trees.

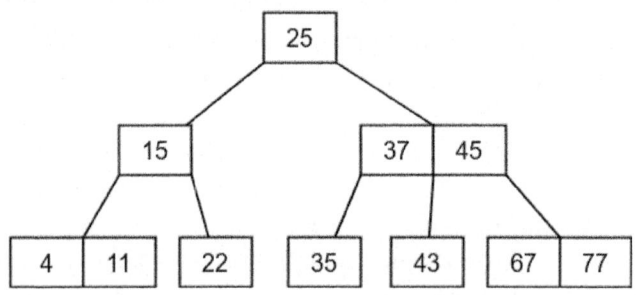

Fig. 7.6: B-Tree of order three

This is an example of a third order B-Tree. You can see that one node can have a maximum of three child-nodes and that each node has one more child than it has keys. When we want to find a value, we exactly know where to navigate to. Look at the right sub-tree for example: If we are looking for a number that is smaller than 37, we go to the left. If we are looking for a number larger than 45, we go right. And if the number is right in between, we go to the middle.

INSERTING ELEMENTS

But what happens when we insert an element into the B-Tree? If the tree is empty, we just make the new element the root node. If it is not empty, we navigate to the position it belongs to. For example, if we were to insert the value 42 into our tree, we would go right first and then into the middle. We would then place it into the same block that the element 43 is in. Since we can have two keys in one block, that is fine.

But what would happen if we would insert the value 80 for example? Of course we would go right two times but then we would have to place it into the same block as 67 and 77. But this would result in a block, which contains three elements and that is not allowed. Because of that, we would then go ahead and push the median value (in this case 77) up one level. After that we would split the block below, make 67 the left child of 77 and 80 the right child of 77. However, you can see that we have the next problem there. We now have three keys on the second level and need to perform another split. Again, we push the median (45 this time) up one level into the root node. The sub-tree with 37 as its root node becomes the left child and the sub-tree with 77 as its root node becomes the right child. In the figure down below, you can see what this process looks like.

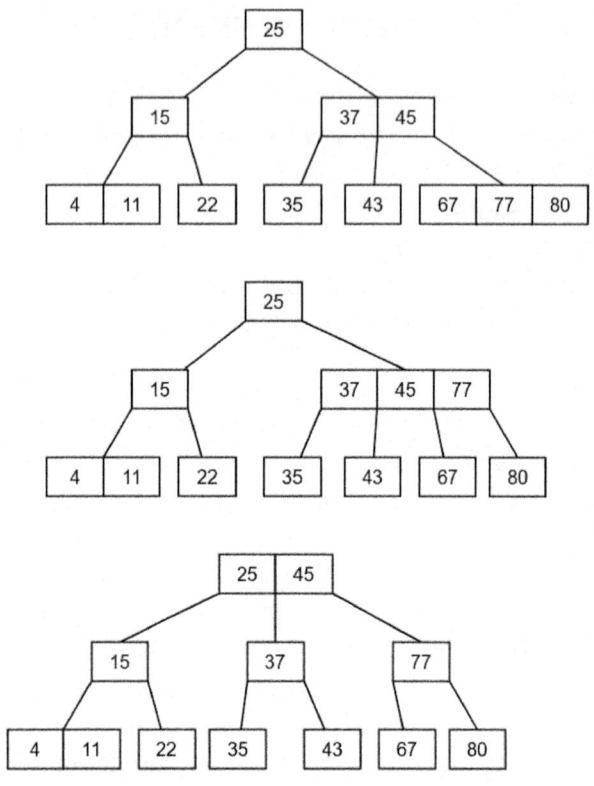

Fig. 7.7: Inserting element into B-Tree

After performing these steps, our tree will always be balanced. All we are doing is putting new elements where they belong and if a block gets too full, we push up its median key. Sometimes this will result in additional levels of height but in general B-Trees are growing in width much more than in height.

The runtime complexity of the insert operation in B-Trees is obviously logarithmic. Since the tree is always balanced, we can navigate to the correct location in logarithmic time. If the list is too full, we need to push up the median one level. In the worst case, this can happen as many times as there are levels in the tree. Therefore this is also possible in logarithmic time.

$$O(\log n)$$

DELETING ELEMENTS

Now let's look at what happens when we delete elements from our B-Tree. Well, if we can delete a key without violating any of the B-Tree definitions, we can just go ahead and do it. Let's say for example, we have a leaf node with two keys in a third order B-Tree. If we want to delete one of the two keys, we can do it without any special operations. The leaf nodes are still all at the same level, we did not exceed the maximum amount of keys per node and we don't have any other limitations for leaf nodes.

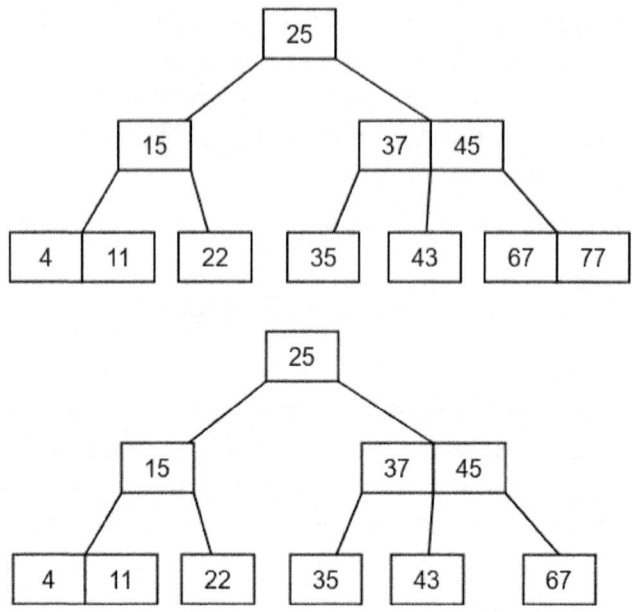

Fig. 7.8: Simple deletion of a leaf-node key (77)

This is the trivial scenario. But what happens when we violate one of the rules and destroy the balance of our tree? Then of course we need to rebalance it.

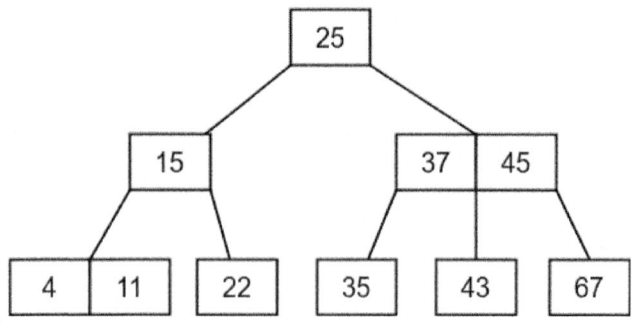

Fig. 7.9: Sample B-Tree for deletion

Look at this tree for example. What would happen if we remove 22? Clearly, we cannot just delete it since 15 would have only one child then and this violates the B-Tree rules. So what we do here is we rotate the values. The value 15 replaces the value 22 and the value 11 takes on the parent node and replaces 15.

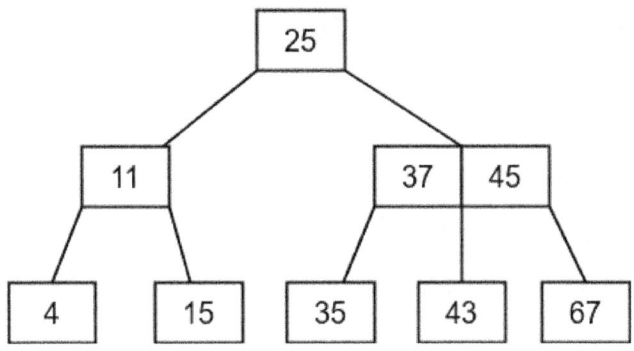

Fig. 7.10: Resulting tree after deletion

Of course the rotation works in the same way if we have two keys in the right child and remove the left one. But then again we can encounter another problem. What if we don't have two keys in the sibling node but only one? In the figure above for example, we could just go ahead and remove 15. The rotation we did before would not work here. We don't have enough keys for it. Because of that, we rotate in a different way and combine 4 and 11 into a single node.

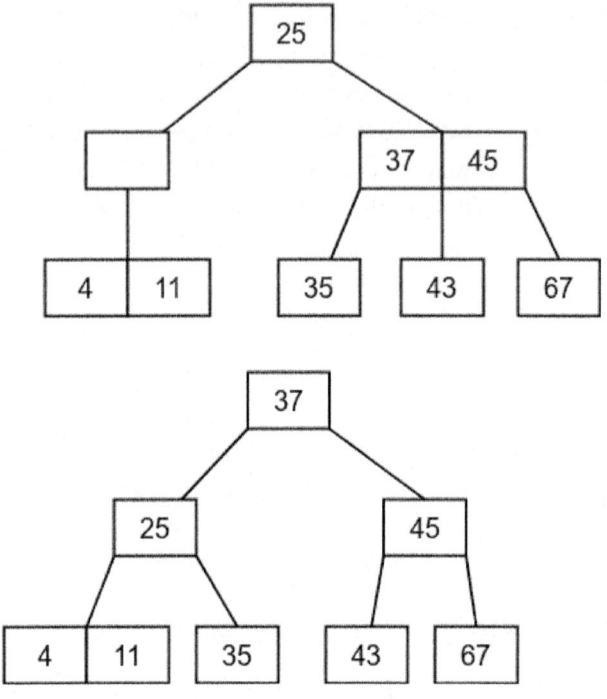

Fig. 7.11: Resulting tree after rotation

You will notice one more problem however. The parent of this node is empty. Thus we need to borrow a key from its sibling and replace the root node with it. Notice that the left child of the right sub-tree node becomes the right child of the left sub-tree node then.

Generally speaking we always fill up gaps either by rotating and borrowing from the sibling nodes or by pushing keys up from child nodes. Similar to insertion, the deletion of elements in B-Trees is also possible in logarithmic time. As you can see, B-Trees are very efficient and like in AVL trees, all major operations have a logarithmic worst-case runtime complexity. On top of that, their block structure is super helpful and beneficial when we work with slow external storage media, since it allows us to minimize the amount accesses.

B*-TREE

Last but not least in this chapter we will look at *B*-*Trees* (pronounced "B star trees"), which are a special variation of B-Trees. The major difference to those is that all the data is contained in the leaf nodes. All the values that come before the leaf layer are just used for navigation.

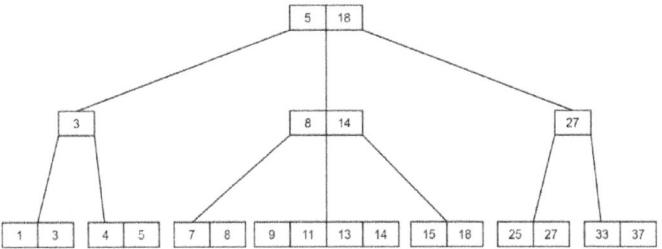

Fig. 7.12: B*-Tree example

The value of the navigation key is always the largest key of its left child node. The amount of the keys in the leaf node is determined by the parameter called *k**. In our leaf node we can have k* to 2k* elements. The tree above has the parameters *m = 3* and *k* = 2* and therefore the leaf nodes can either have two, three or four keys.

RUNTIME COMPLEXITIES

The runtime complexities for searching, inserting and deleting are the same as for normal B-Trees. However, in B*-Trees we always need to go to the leaf nodes in order to access data. This doesn't change the average number of steps needed though, since B*-Trees usually have a smaller height than ordinary B-Trees.

In general, B-Trees and B*-Trees are oftentimes used in database systems and file systems. Their logarithmic runtime complexity and their block structure are perfect for these fields.

Of course there are also many more tree data structures with a different set of advantages and disadvantages. If you are looking for exotic data structures, you will have to use your favorite search engine to explore these. In this book we have covered the most important of them and we will now head into the last chapter, which is about the extremely exciting topic of *hashing*.

8 – HASHING

You have probably heard of *hashing* in the context of passwords and cyber security already. Almost always when you sign up for an account online, your clear text password is hashed and transformed into a string that cannot be deciphered. This string is then saved and whenever you try to log into your account, the password that you try to log in with will also be hashed and compared to the hash stored in the database. If they match, you are granted access.

In contrast to encryption, hashing is a one-way street. You cannot "dehash" a string into the original clear text password. This is obviously true, because different inputs may produce the same hash (even though it is very unlikely to happen using most hashing algorithms).

But why are we talking about this cyber security topic in a book on algorithms and data structures? Well, hashing is not only used for passwords but also for an efficient way to access data. Instead of looking for values in a huge dataset by comparing keys, we can arithmetically calculate their positions. You can think about this like a telephone book. Each initial letter of a name could have its own page. Then we could define a *hash function*, which we could use to calculate the position of any entry.

$$h(s) = ord(s[0])$$

In this case, the parameter *s* would be the name of the person, we want to either save or look up. The *ord* function we are using here just gives us a numerical value for each initial letter. For this example, we will assume that the letter *A* has the value zero, the letter *B* has the value one and so on.

0 ("A")	Anna 432, Angela 787
1 ("B")	Bob 892
2 ("C")	
3 ("D")	Dora 990, Daniel 211
4 ("E")	
5 ("F")	
6 ("G")	
7 ("H")	Henry 232
...	...
25 ("Z")	

We can now go ahead and create a so-called *hash table* based on the ideas we just discussed. Whenever we want to add or look up a name and the associated number, we can just calculate the position instead of navigating to it using comparisons. For example, if we wanted to add the number of a person named *Gerald*, we would feed the name into our hash function and it would return the position or index six.

But you have probably already noticed the problem here. There are many people that have the same name, let alone the same starting letter. This means that we will experience many so-called *collisions.* A collision happens when two different inputs result in the same hash. We cannot store two different numbers at the same address.

Hashing is an operation that can be done in constant time, but this is only the case, if we have a negligible amount of collisions. If we don't have an intelligent way of dealing with collisions, we could end up with a worst-case complexity that is linear. And since inserting, deleting and searching are fully based on hashing here, this is very important. So for this chapter, we will focus on two major questions:

- What are good hash functions?
- How can we resolve collisions efficiently?

We will start by briefly talking about two types of hash functions first. When we have talked about those, we will also take a look at how to intelligently minimize the likelihood of collisions and also at how to minimize the amount of steps needed to resolve these, when they happen.

HASH FUNCTIONS

Before we actually talk about specific hash functions, let us ask the question of what characterizes a good hash function. What are we expecting from it? There are two major properties that a good hash function absolutely needs to have. The first one is that all possible inputs or keys are distributed as evenly as possible to all positions of the hash table. And the second one is that even tiny changes in the inputs shall produce significantly different hashes.

Have you ever tried to play around with major hashing algorithms like SHA-256? Try entering a password like "ilovecake", look at the hash and then try entering a slightly different password like "ilovecakes". The hash is completely different, even though the input was almost the same. That is a characteristic of a good hash function.

DIVISION METHOD

The first hash function that we will look at is the so-called *division method*. Here we take the input and calculate the remainder of a division by a number *m*.

$$h(k) = k \bmod m$$

For this we assume that *k* is a natural number. This hash function allows for a rapid calculation of the hashes. However, it is extremely important that the value for *m* is chosen intelligently. A good choice for *m* is a prime number. Very bad choices would be powers of two or ten for example.

Even though *k* has to be a number for this calculation to work, we can easily apply that function to strings as well. All we need to do for that is to treat the individual characters as numbers and multiply them with a proper factor.

MULTIPLICATION METHOD

Alternatively, we can also use the *multiplication method*. Here we use an irrational number A and multiply it to our key. After that we subtract the integer part of the result. This means that we end up with a number between one and zero. Then last but not least we go ahead, multiply the result by the size of the table m and floor it.

$$h(k) = \lfloor m(k * A - \lfloor k * A \rfloor) \rfloor$$

This method gives us an even distribution of our values. The choice of the variable m is not critical as long as A is an irrational number. The perfect value for A is the so-called *golden ratio*, which is approximately 0.6180339887. A formula for this ratio is the following:

$$A = \phi^{-1} = \frac{\sqrt{5} - 1}{2}$$

Of course you can also choose other irrational numbers for A, like the square root of two or pi.

COLLISION RESOLUTION

Whatever hash function we choose, there will always be the possibility of two different inputs producing the same hash. And since our functions are not as complex as the SHA-256 algorithm for example, this might happen quite often. That is only a problem however, if we don't handle those collisions intelligently. So let's look at some different ways in which we could resolve collisions.

SEPARATE CHAINING

The first method we will look at is called *separate chaining*. In this case, each element of the hash table is a linked list, where the first entry points to the second one, the second one points to the third one and so on.

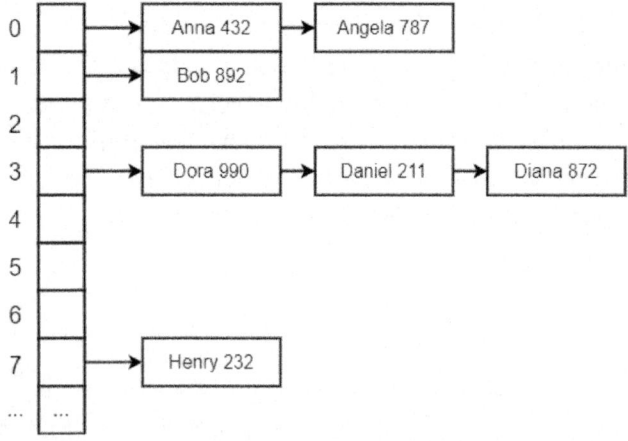

Fig. 8.1: Separate chaining

So when we want to enter an element into our hash table, we have two possible scenarios. If the hash of our element occurs for the first time, we just create a new linked list and the inserted element becomes its head. If we get to a position or hash that was already used before, we append the new element to the linked list. When we then go ahead and look for a certain element in our hash table, we will have to iterate through all nodes that come before it.

Open Addressing

An alternative method for collision handling is the so-called *open addressing.* Here we directly save our data in an ordinary array. Additionally we also save one flag per position that can have one out of three states. Let's call those *free, occupied* and *free again.* What we do when we encounter a collision is we look at other possible positions in a specific order. This is called *probing.*

0 ("A")	Anna 432	Occupied
1 ("B")	Angela 787	Occupied
2 ("C")		Free
3 ("D")	Dora 990	Occupied
4 ("E")		Free
5 ("F")		Free
6 ("G")		Free
7 ("H")	Henry 232	Occupied
...	...	...
25 ("Z")		Free

In the table above you can see, that *Angela* is actually at the position reserved for the starting letter *B*. This is the case because we first wanted to insert it at position *A* but this position was already occupied by *Anna*. Therefore we just took the next position that was free. If we now were to insert the name and number of *Bob*, we would try the position *B* first but then go to position *C*, since *B* is already occupied and *C* is the next one that is free.

Now you might be asking yourself what we need the flag *free again* for. Let's think about this. What happens if we want to find *Angela* in our hash table? We would hash the initial letter and end up at index zero. There we would find *Anna* and thus proceed to the next position, which is index one and find *Angela*. If we look for some name that doesn't exist, like *Arnold* for example, we would sooner or later end up at a *free* position and know that the name will not be found.

But what happens when we delete *Anna* for example? If we just set the flag to *free*, there is no way we could find *Angela*. When we hash the initial letter *A*, we would get to index zero, see that it is free and stop searching. However, if we set it to *free again*, we can put new values there but at the same time we know that we can continue looking for values that ended up in different positions due to collisions.

This example is pretty trivial but it gives you an understanding of the general idea behind probing and open addressing. Some of the algorithms we will look at next use more sophisticated methods for determining the next position to look at.

LINEAR PROBING

Linear probing for example adds an additional parameter to our hash function. This parameter is called *i* and indicates how many collisions we have experienced already.

$$h(k, i) = (h'(k) + i) \bmod m$$

As you can see, the final hash function is composed of a simple hash function called *h'(k)* and two additional values. We always add *i* to the result of our hash function and then calculate the remainder of a division by *m*. Since we don't have any collisions in the beginning, in the first iteration *i* is zero and can be ignored. For each collision we encounter, we increase the value of *i* by one. Let's look at an example.

$$m = 8, \ h'(k) = k \bmod m$$

Inserted values for k	10	19	31	22	14	16
Resulting hashes of h'(k)	2	3	7	6	6	0

We have a hash table size of *m = 8* and we are inserting the values above into the table in that exact order. So first we insert ten and the resulting hash for that value is two. Therefore we place it at index two. We do the same thing for the other values as well. But as you can see, 22 and 14 result in the same hash. When we divide those two numbers by eight, both have a remainder of six. So now we have to resolve this collision.

$$h(14, 1) = (h'(14) + 1) \bmod 8 = 7 \bmod 8 = 7$$

The next position we shall look at is seven. But this position is already occupied by 31. So we increase *i* by one and repeat the last calculation.

$$h(14,2) = (h'(14) + 2) \bmod 8 = 8 \bmod 8 = 0$$

Now we found an index that was not used before and we can place the value 14 there. However, the number 16 also has a hash value of zero. Therefore we apply the same process here and it ends up at position number one. The final hash table looks like this:

0	1	2	3	4	5	6	7
14	16	10	19			22	31

Essentially, all we are doing is always just looking at the next position. That's why it is called linear probing. But there are some problems with this approach. The probability for the different positions to be the result of the hash function is not the same. Whenever we insert an element at a certain position we change the probability for the next position to be the result of the hash function. This means that long occupied parts of the hash table are more likely to grow than short parts. This drastically decreases the efficiency of our collision handling.

The ideal form of hashing that we would like to have is called *uniform hashing*. There, every key has the same likelihood of getting any of the *m! (Factorial)* permutations of the positions as its probing order. However, it is extremely difficult to implement this in reality and because of that we approximate this with the following procedures.

QUADRATIC PROBING

In order to counteract the problems we experienced with linear probing, *quadratic probing* chooses the next positions to look at with a quadratically increasing distance.

$$h(k, i) = (h'(k) + c_1 i + c_2 i^2) \bmod m$$

This time we choose two constants c_1 and c_2, which add not only a value based on *i* but also on *i squared*. So when we experience a collision, we don't just look at the next position but at a position that is farther away probably. Then if we encounter a second collision, we don't take the same step size to look for a next position but we increase the step size quadratically.

This counteracts the problem of *primary clustering* that we talked about. However, it creates the similar problem of *secondary clustering*. Definitely better than linear probing but not optimal.

DOUBLE HASHING

We can almost get to the efficiency of uniform hashing if we use a second hashing function instead of random permutations. This is the approach called *double hashing*. We define two functions h_1 and h_2 and combine them into a final hash function, which includes the factor *i* as well.

$$h(k, i) = (h_1(k) + h_2(k) * i) \bmod m$$

Now the factor with which we multiply i is not the same constant for all inputs but a value that is actually based on the key. This approach is way better than quadratic probing and in practice it has almost the same efficiency as the ideal of uniform hashing.

WHAT'S NEXT?

You can be very proud of yourself if you have read the whole book until the end. The topic of algorithms and data structures is extremely complex and by most considered to be one of the hardest subjects in computer science. In this book I tried to give you an intuitive understanding of this complex field. If you understood most of the concepts in this book, you have progressed tremendously in your programming career. As I already mentioned in the beginning of this book, most major tech companies will ask you questions related to algorithms and data structures in their job interviews. These skills are fundamental to every sub-field of computer science. In cyber security and ethical hacking, in machine learning, in game development, in enterprise applications – literally everywhere. So even though it is (or in your case *was*) hard, it will definitely pay off for you and I am glad that you made it through this book without giving up.

But now you might be asking: What's next? What is the next step on your journey to becoming a better programmer? Well, it depends on what your goals are. If this book ignited the passion for more abstract concepts, you might be interested in learning even more about algorithms and data structures. There are much more complex topics like dynamic programming, P and NP problems, approximation etc. If you are interested in more content focusing on algorithms let me know by either contacting me on social media (YouTube or Instagram: NeuralNine) or by leaving an Amazon review. I will definitely release a second and maybe even third part, if there is enough demand for it.

However, maybe you are not interested in more algorithms and you want to learn more about practical programming with Python for example. In this case, I can highly recommend you to check out my book series on Python programming, especially if you enjoyed this book. On my website you can find all seven volumes, which take you from complete beginner, through intermediate concepts, data science, machine learning, finance programming and neural networks up until the interesting field of computer vision. Check those out if you are interested.

Link to books: https://www.neuralnine.com/books

Alternatively or additionally you can also become a subscriber of my YouTube channel for free. There I post a lot of tutorials and programming projects on a regular basis. You can find tutorials on databases, TCP chats, DDOS scripts, stock visualizations and much more. I would be happy to see you there.

YouTube link: https://www.youtube.com/c/NeuralNine

Instagram link: https://www.instagram.com/NeuralNine

Last but not least I want to thank you for reading this book and to ask you for a tiny favor. If you enjoyed this book and it benefited your career, please leave a positive review on Amazon to help other people make the same choice as you. The reviews on Amazon are tremendously important when it comes to the buying decisions. If you want to help me as well as my community to grow, please spare two minutes to write a short review on Amazon. Thank you very much!

I wish you a lot of success on your journey!

https://www.neuralnine.com/books

Printed in Great Britain
by Amazon